MW00817970

Groaning

Grace + Peace

Warren M. Bailey

GROANING

Sounds in Search of a Witness

Warner M. Bailey

CASCADE *Books* · Eugene, Oregon

GROANING
Sounds in Search of a Witness

Copyright © 2023 Warner M. Bailey. All rights reserved. Except for brief
quotations in critical publications or reviews, no part of this book may
be reproduced in any manner without prior written permission from the
publisher. Write: Permissions, Wipf and Stock Publishers, 199 W. 8th Ave.,
Suite 3, Eugene, OR 97401.

Cascade Books
An Imprint of Wipf and Stock Publishers
199 W. 8th Ave., Suite 3
Eugene, OR 97401

www.wipfandstock.com

PAPERBACK ISBN: 978-1-6667-3775-2
HARDCOVER ISBN: 978-1-6667-9757-2
EBOOK ISBN: 978-1-6667-9758-9

Cataloguing-in-Publication data:

Names: Bailey, Warner M. [author]
Title: Groaning : sounds in search of a witness / Warner M. Bailey.
Description: Eugene, OR: Cascade Books, 2023 | Includes bibliographical
references.
Identifiers: ISBN 978-1-6667-3775-2 (paperback) | ISBN 978-1-6667-9757-2
(hardcover) | ISBN 978-1-6667-9758-9 (ebook)
Subjects: LCSH: Suffering—Religious aspects—Christianity. | Laments—
History and criticism. | Bible—Lamentations—Criticism, interpreta-
tions, etc. | Black theology. | Black people—Religion.
Classification: BT732.7 B35 2023 (print) | BT732.7 (ebook)

FEBRUARY 13, 2023 9:20 AM

To Joanna Marie Bailey
Beloved Daughter and Hospital Chaplain
whose presence as a witness to "sighs too deep for words"
is a ministry of healing.

CONTENTS

Introduction

When, at the end of May 2020, a white Minneapolis police officer riveted his knee into the neck of George Floyd and pushed the air out of him, that cop scarred the American consciousness with a searing symbol of the injustices that Black men and women have submitted to since their coming to these shores in the seventeenth century. That cop may have thought he was just doing his job. However, what he did will be forever a symbol of a structure of white supremacy deeply rooted in our nation, despite relentless efforts to be rid of it. The policeman's knee to the neck of Mr. Floyd preserves simultaneously both profound suffering and callous domination. The power of the symbol outstrips the ability of words to express and convulses viewers—Black and white—in groaning.

This book comes out of that incident, which reverberated all over the world. Even as I was reeling from the ugly shock of this symbol, I began to listen as a pastor to reactions to the crime. I noted how frequently and over a wide range of settings did persons use the word "groaning" to describe their emotional response to the impact of the murder of George Floyd. This resonated deeply with my response. As part of how I coped with what I was feeling, I wanted to understand this visceral response better. I took heart that others thought this reaction was worthy of deeper understanding, too. The *New York Times* columnist David Brooks devoted a full opinion piece to it. In this introduction, I tell something of my journey.

I am very grateful to David J. Gouwens for guiding me early in my journey to the philosophical theologian Robert C. Roberts. Reading his work, I deepened my impression that groaning was not irrational noise but a genuine emotion that carried a massive burden of concern. Roberts supplied a way of responding to groaning through the process of contextualizing and transforming its burden of concern within a framework of hope.

With this validation of the integrity of groaning, I launched my inquiry as a biblical scholar into the textual evidence for groaning and how it was contextualized and transformed. My investigation soon led me to the book of Lamentations, where groaning plays a pivotal role in Lamentations 1. This literary record presents opportunities to reflect on what happens to people when they suffer the complete collapse of a worldview, how they cope both with profound upheaval of their daily living and the shattering of their spiritual and symbolic world. Being guided initially by the work of Kathleen O'Connor and Robin Parry, I soon realized that the role of the witness to groaning was indispensable to the relief of the groaning one. My study of Lamentations, chiefly chapter 1, made very clear how groaning could be looked at as sounds in search of a witness. "Look and see if there is any sorrow like my sorrow!" (Lam 1:12). A witness both validates the personhood of the groaner and can be a point of redress for the groaner. Here emerged for me the possibilities for engaging again the causes of such profound suffering.

This insight led me to the theological problem of Lamentations, the silence of God, the non-responsiveness of God as witness. I argue that the silence of God is crystallized in the symbol of God as the anti-shepherd who terrorized the flock of Israel in exile by silence in Lamentations 1. The poems of Lamentations reflect a collection of voices in Israel attempting to make sense of this silence. The book contains a range of opinions, including but not limited to the ideas that suffering is the penalty for transgression, or Israel's suffering is punitive and excessive, or God does not willingly cause suffering. The ending of the book, "If you have utterly rejected us, and are angry with us beyond measure, then . . ."

(Lam 5:22), presents a stark, impending reality of baleful, divine rejection.

Yet, God does not intend for this to be the final result. The portion of the book of Isaiah commonly referred to as Second Isaiah, beginning with chapter 40, mounts an almost point-by-point response to the possibility of final rejection. God makes the Suffering Servant of Isa 52–53 to be the witness that corresponds to the suffering of Lamentations. By God's intentional commission, he mirrors human suffering and stands as God's sufficient witness to human groaning. Much of what Lamentations cries out to be noted and relieved is met in Second Isaiah.

I pursue the Servant as witness into the story of how Jesus expands this witness into the symbol of his resurrected body that bears the wounds of his suffering and abandonment.[1] His open wounds invite us to see him as the universally sufficient witness who accompanies us with our scars into a future that has integrity and honor. I am grateful for the fruitful conversations I had with my colleague Timothy Sandoval in coming to the conclusions I share.

I was not content to let the collection of profoundly disturbing responses to the murder of George Floyd be simply an anecdotal introduction to the study of Lamentations, however. To do so would have the result of my co-opting their suffering for a narrowly personal end. It would stand as one more instance of a white man using Black trauma for personal gain. Explicating the biblical notion of a witness raised by Lamentations makes me, the interpreter, now a witness, a participant in the groaning observed, though never from an equivalent perspective. Even so, as a witness, the horizon of my work reaches out to Black readers of Scripture whose interpretation of the sacred text is informed by Black religious experience. Whatever constructive thoughts I have must be forged in conversation with them.

A brief word about my perspective is required. I grew up as a white male in the Jim Crow South and I benefitted from that

---

1. See the process of symbol-making involving Incipient, Discursive, and Dynamic stages, as used by "post-traumatic literary intervention" in survivor literature, in O'Connor, "How Trauma Studies," 213.

oppressive system. I was trained as a Reformed theologian and biblical interpreter, and I led Presbyterian congregations for forty years. From this perspective I have sought to understand and appreciate the work of James Cone, James Evers, Eddie Glaude Jr., and M. Shawn Copeland. These thought leaders have been honest and caring guides to appreciating the wide range of Black religious thinking. I came away with a much better understanding of the existential stakes in African Americans maintaining integrity against an oppressive system into which I was born and from which I benefited. I gained a better appreciation of how these leaders shaped their theologies of survival against this system. In their capable hands, the figure of the witness took various shapes, but they all insisted that a witness must be engaged in order to press on toward freedom, even as centuries-old scars were borne. Conversations with David Gouwens and Ed Waggoner contributed to greater clarity of understanding.

America is smothered by multiple traumas. In addition to the continuing trauma of racial injustice, people are scarred by domestic terror, the trauma of climate change, COVID-19 pandemic, and the trauma of moral injury after war that afflicts both military personnel and civilians. Now is added the war of Russian aggression in Ukraine. These and other traumas all cry out for a witness. We live in a company of grief.

In the final chapter I discuss various ways to harness the power of groaning as it is christologically contextualized and transformed. Within the arena of the eschatological power held by the crucified Christ groaning becomes a powerful witness to suffering and a spur to advocacy for its relief. I imagine how Lamentations in its canonical setting can support the church being a safe space to groan together in the presence of powerful resources in text, ritual, and hospitality, all of which hold promise for forward movement, carrying our scars.

This chapter owes a debt of gratitude to conversations with pastoral theologians Nancy J. Ramsay and Barbara McClure. A result of these conversations is an exploration of how Lamentations 1 can be employed as a resource for the care of those who have been morally injured by war. Simply stated, this book offers encouragement and insight to pastoral leaders of congregations in their mission to provide renewal to exhausted and groaning persons by shaping a future in which they can thrive spiritually, even as they carry their scars.

The powerful voices of Black theologians continue to press the point that the goal of this study is not the management of groaning such that it ensures passivity in the face of domination, but rather, the empowerment of the groaner to struggle for liberation from oppressive structures and systems. Likewise, as the healing from moral injury requires former aggressors moving beyond the shattering of commonly accepted notions of national exceptionalism and divine omnipotence, so a similar shattering of the notions of supremacy is required, along with the construction of a new way of self-understanding, if the powerful who become attentive to the groans of Black persons are to be effective partners. This book makes the claim that the crucified Jesus now resurrected is an effective structure of meaning through which to make this conversion.

I am profoundly indebted to Michael Miller for sharing generously his time for conversation throughout the time I was writing this book. He has followed closely my manuscript in its development and has offered cogent suggestions and constant encouragement.

I am indebted to Jill Duffield, former editor of the *Presbyterian Outlook,* for publishing an early attempt at expressing my thoughts in an article, "'I Can't Breathe,' The Racist Assault upon the Breath of God," October 26, 2020, 22–27, and to Terri McDowell Ott, current editor of the *Outlook,* for publishing an excerpt from chapters 3 and 4, "The Return of the Shepherd-God," May 1, 2022, 22–27.

I dedicate this book to my daughter, the Reverend Joanna Marie Bailey, in recognition of her long and distinguished service as a hospital chaplain in both patient-facing and managerial roles. Her unwavering commitment to being a witness to the groans of those who are sick and dying while also ministering to the health of stressed coworkers, especially during this ongoing pandemic, calls forth gratitude from her parents and praise from her colleagues.

Finally and most fervently, I express my gratitude to my wife, Mary, who has helped me in more ways that I can describe through searching conversations that come out of her heart that deeply cares.

Chapter 1

LISTENING TO VOICES IN PAIN

H OW DO YOU MAKE meaning when you run out of words? How do you reach out and unburden yourself when your thesaurus is empty? It's not that you have nothing more to say. Rather, the enormity of what you are struggling to communicate overpowers your ability to find the right words to convey that burden. You even struggle to find words to describe what happens to you when you cannot talk about what you want to talk about.

It is strange and unnerving to discover, suddenly, that you have run out of words. Especially for a church that is founded upon the Word of God, a church where words are principal conduits through which flow the life of the church. However, these are highly unusual times. You only have to listen intently, and you will hear all sorts of people speaking about running out of words to talk about the impact of a multilayered concatenation of traumatizing shocks upon the fabric of our common lives. I make no claim to completeness, but I've heard enough to convince me that, at least when it comes to talking about being a victim of white supremacy, or a victim of systemic lying, or a victim of cultural betrayal, we can run out of words. I begin with a survey of national responses to the death of George Floyd while in police custody.

A most poignant response and penetrating analysis comes in an essay submitted to *Time* magazine (May 29, 2020) by Eddie S. Glaude Jr., the James S. McDonnell Distinguished University

Professor and chair of the Department of African American Studies at Princeton University.[1] Overwhelmed by the monstrosity of Floyd's death, Glaude asks the unanswerable question:

> How does one live in such a time? What happens in your bones, on your insides, when you're ravaged by disease and hatred? For those African-Americans who have lost loved ones and their jobs, who find themselves in long lines at food banks, who have to deal with the ongoing stress of a virus that can strike at any moment, how do you manage the trauma of loss and the terror of seeing another Black person killed by the police?

The trauma of watching the video of Floyd's death is searing:

> Minneapolis police officer Derek Chauvin had his knee pinned against Floyd's neck for close to eight minutes. We heard a haunting repetition of the words "I can't breathe." Floyd cried out for his deceased mother and called out for his children as he desperately clung to life. Chauvin sat there, smug, hand in his pocket, with little regard for the man dying underneath the pressure of his knee. All of this over someone allegedly trying to use a counterfeit twenty-dollar bill at a local deli.

We hear the frustration building up as Glaude puts this horrendous death into historical context:

> Even if you turn your head away, the images and the sounds continue to haunt. We play them over and over again. It's part of a ritual practice, a way the nation manages its racist sins. People declare their outrage. . . . They cry for justice. Or, as in the past, . . . they defend the police. They condemn the violence. Wash. Rinse. Repeat. And nothing changes.

The unanswerable questions compounded by repeatable traumatizing memory in the context of frustration over the seeming pointlessness of national response precipitates exhaustion and groaning:

1. Glaude, "George Floyd's Murder." I have revised slightly the order of some paragraphs to emphasize the subject of my investigation.

I watched the Floyd video and completely lost it. The stress of the times combined with the cruelty of the act and Floyd's desperate plea broke me. I found myself, which I rarely do, burying my head into my hands. Weeping. I thought about all the Black people who may watch the video in the middle of this pandemic and about the white people who would see it and ask the all-too-familiar questions about how do we change.

This essay was accompanied by an interview with NPR correspondent Amna Nazaw on May 29, 2020, and subsequently published by *Time* on June 15, 2020.[2] In the interview, Glaude points to how the unanswered questions are the grounds for anger:

But I do want to say this, though, that is anger is—the anger that was expressed over the last few days, and especially last night, reflects, I think, a kind of accumulated grievance, you know?

And in the way in which we tell the story of African-American politics, we always want to kind of bracket anger. We're not allowed to be angry in public. And, in some ways, anger, going back to the ancients, going all the way back to Aristotle, announces that something just happened here.

It puts folk on notice that something must change. And it's not just simply a spontaneous act. It is the consequence of, shall we say, as I said earlier, accumulated grievances.

Glaude's only way to express his mounting frustration was by groaning.

And you use the word "another" because we have seen video after video. What's the collective impact of that, the cumulative toll of those videos?

Oh, my God. I mean, for those of us who have to watch it, and then we have to worry about our children and our brothers and sisters and our uncles and aunts and

2. Glaude, "We Cannot Wait."

friends, right, it increases the levels of stress and worry and concern.

So, here we are in the moment in which we're dealing with a global pandemic, trying to figure out how to live under these conditions. And we still have to deal with the fact that our children, that our family members, that our friends can be murdered by the police.

It makes living hard. It makes it difficult, in a moment that's already difficult and hard.

He cried out for his mother.

She's been dead for two years. She's been dead. He basically told someone to tell my kids that I love them, because I'm going to die.

And that man, that moral monster kept his knee on his neck.

I didn't—I couldn't process it. It broke me.

The unanswerable questions compounded by repeatable traumatizing memory in the context of frustration over the seeming pointlessness of national response precipitates exhaustion and groaning. We are stuck as much by Glaude's candor as by the monstrosity of the outrageous act. Weeping is Glaude's only outlet to convey the burden of the trauma his thoughts were carrying.

Trauma and the language of trauma is a major theme of this book. Therefore, it will be helpful to state a working definition of trauma and its effects on language.

A general understanding of trauma holds that a person can be overwhelmed by disastrous events such that they are unable to absorb violent events as they happen.[3] These events ingrain themselves neurotically in a person's character as recurring memories to haunt the traumatized. Because these memories keep overwhelming them, victims can rarely speak about traumatic violence. "Language fractures and breaks down so people are unable to express their experiences, leaving them bereft and isolated."[4] As this book progresses, it will become clear how groaning is a form of this fracturing of language. Because language is a major factor in forming

3. See Dietrich, "Cultural Traumata in the Ancient Near East," 145.

4. O'Connor, "How Trauma Studies," 213.

meaning, any breakdown of language produces a consequent breakdown in the structure of beliefs that once supported life.

The footage of the execution of George Floyd's murder quickly became a national symbol of the four-centuries-old grip of white supremacy. The impact of this symbol has rippled across our nation. We turn now to a collection of instances of its effect.

Two examples from the Miami-based national syndicated columnist Leonard Pitts begin to fill out the picture of groaning. Early in the summer of 2020, he put his finger on it.

> We are living through a year without historic parallel. Or maybe it's more accurate to say it's a year with too much historic parallel. It's like a mashup of history's greatest hits, 1918 (the flu pandemic) meets 1929 (the Great Depression) meets, well . . . take you pick: 1943 (uprising in Harlem over police brutality); 1965 (uprising in Watts over police brutality); 1980 (uprising in Miami over police brutality); 1992 (uprising in LA over police brutality), to name only a few. Any one of those—a pandemic, a depression or an uprising—would define a pretty tough year. This year has given us all three at once. And it's only June. . . . People are exhausted, angry, on edge, exhausted, frightened, frustrated, exhausted, confused, troubled, and exhausted.[5]

Exhausted, crushed. Subjected to such a constant hammering, what words can you reach for to tell about how you are feeling, what you are thinking? There aren't any, Pitts goes on to say, offering instead the encouragement to watch professional sports, in this case, basketball. Seriously.

> Because here's the thing: In this angry, edgy, frightening, frustrating, confusing, troubling, and exhausting moment, I'm sure I speak for more than just myself when I say that I need to scream at a number that's only a score, not a death toll, need to groan over something that's only a missed free throw, not a vanishing 401(k). . . . We are all bent under a load of this singular, awful, year.

5. Pitts, "The Distraction of Basketball."

Screaming. Groaning. That's all you have left when you've run out of words to express "this angry, edgy, frightening, frustrating, confusing, troubling, and exhausting moment."

But the context of our collective trauma runs thicker. Again, the analysis of Pitts, which he published at the end of this summer, is spot-on. "Trump's untruths have become not simply normal, but taken for granted. The sheer volume of his lies seems to keep any one of them from mattering all that much. . . . There is so much. . . . One's ability to be indignant—or even to pay attention—is simply overwhelmed. . . . All lies matter, so no lies matter."

Speaking of former President Trump's admission to Bob Woodward that he deliberately deceived the American public about COVID-19, Pitts observes,

> But one doubts any of us will be surprised, or even truly outraged. We have lost something—the ability to expect recognizable adult, human behavior in our leader. Worse, we've also lost what we said we wouldn't: the ability to feel disappointed and indignant when it does not come. There is an element of exhaustion here. Fury feels rote, less a feeling than the memory of one.[6]

There's that mention of exhaustion, again, and, now, its consequences of being overwhelmed and a troubling loss of vigor, genuineness, and quick response.[7] But there's more this time around. Pitts points to how the exhaustion created by Trump's behavior has had the effect of wiping away from the public's mind the ability to expect someone to perform at commonly held standards of presidential leadership. If the issue involved a standard commonly held, we would have the words. Because, however, commonly held expectations have been wiped away, we search our dictionaries in

6. Pitts, "Trump's Many Lies."

7. From a different perspective, Levine collects research by psychologists and experimental economists showing that "the very fact of scarcity distorts the human decision-making process." Poor people traumatized by systemic poverty suffer from cognitive overload. See *Healing the Reason-Emotion Split*, 62–63.

vain for what to say. The lack of any structure of meaning demolishes language.

To make a short diversion from surveying Black responses, I am struck by how close our situation comes to what Dietrich Bonhoeffer described as national stupidity, which he experienced in Germany's capitulation to the ideology of Nazism. In his presciently retrospective 1942 essay, "After Ten Years," Bonhoeffer, a Lutheran theologian who would be hanged for his part in the plot to assassinate Adolf Hitler, writes "that, under certain circumstances, people are *made* stupid or that they allow this to happen to them." He goes on to explain

> that under the overwhelming impact of rising power, humans are deprived of their inner independence and, more or less consciously, give up establishing an autonomous position toward the emerging circumstances. . . . In conversation with [the stupid person] one virtually feels that one is dealing not at all with him as a person, but with slogans, catchwords, and the like that have taken possession of him. He is under a spell, blinded, misused, and abused in his very being. Having thus become a mindless tool, the stupid person will also be capable of any evil and at the same time incapable of seeing that it is evil.[8]

This stupidity can only be removed, Bonhoeffer says, by a crushing defeat that shatters the spell and shocks a dormant structure of decency back into life. The collapse of Nazi Germany proved his words presciently correct.

Pitts describes a national scene with telling effect. But other voices add confirmation to his disturbing reflections.

For example, consider Black media mogul Tyler Perry's essay for *People* magazine on the impact of the death of George Floyd, written contemporaneously with Pitts's first opinion column. It was a heartfelt, first-person sharing of his thoughts on racial injustice and police brutality against unarmed Black people in America. Like Pitts, Perry reached for the word "exhausted" to reflect the impact of what he has recently seen across the country.

8. Bonhoeffer, *"After Ten Years,"* 22–23.

"I'm exhausted from all the hate and the division, the vitriol that I see online from one to another. . . . I'm exhausted from seeing these kinds of senseless murders play out over and over again with nothing changing in our society." Focusing on George Floyd, "The level of racism and brutality that George Floyd faced is something that we as Black people know all too well. . . . When I saw that video, *I had so many raw, guttural emotions.* I felt for him and his family. I felt for all of us as Black people. I felt for my five-year-old son."[9] One cannot miss the irony of Perry's admission. This media mogul was reduced to raw, guttural sounds because he ran out of words to carry what he felt.

Another voice surprised me, speaking in the cadences of my home state. During the first weeks of outrage over Mr. Floyd's murder NASCAR competition reopened at the Texas Motor Speedway where I live in Fort Worth, Texas. As was reported nationally, a noose was discovered as a pull for the garage door opener to Bubba Wallace's bay.[10] While subsequent investigation revealed that it had been attached long before the bay was assigned to Wallace, the initial reaction interpreted it to be a racist attack on Wallace, the only Black driver in the race, and someone who had advocated for the removal of the Confederate battle flag at NASCAR-sanctioned races. Since the noose was discovered in an area restricted to drivers and their crews, the attack raised the initial possibility of it being a racist attack from someone within the sport who had access to area.

Immediate response to the discovery was widespread revulsion, resulting in a maximum show of support to Wallace and to the Black Lives Matter movement. National media carried statements from fellow drivers, owners, NASCAR officials, and fans. For our purposes, the reaction from Eddie Gossage, the white Texas Motor Speedway president, is particularly relevant. "I just can't tell you how awful I felt when I saw the news on Sunday night. I can't put it into words and I never struggle with words. It's just, 'C'mon, really? This is the response?' It's just awful. It makes our sport look

9. As reported in the *Fort Worth Star-Telegram*, June 18, 2020, my emphasis.
10. See, for example, *Fort Worth Star-Telegram*, June 28, 2020, 1B.

horrible. For someone clearly within the sport to do this . . . that's just unforgivable." While the garage door pull was easily explained, eventually, Gossage's candid comments are significant in that they provide another illustration of being in a situation where you run out of words. It also is significant that this is being told from the perspective of a white person who is deeply in solidarity with fighting a white-supremacist perception on race-related issues for years in professional racing.

It may seem a long stretch between the heat of a Texas race track to the ivy-covered halls of academia, but Yale physics professor Larry Gladney, who is also dean of diversity and faculty development, conveys similar experiences of "wordlessness" in the wake of George Floyd's death.[11]

> What can anyone say in the face of a devastating and ruinous history that stretches continually from slave patrols to systemic police brutality on black people? Many of my faculty colleagues, who are all accustomed to talking through difficult topics, are at a loss for words to express not merely anger but screaming outrage that these pounding blows to our collective psyche never end. Witnesses, video footage, scholarly research all fail to change the national pattern of no justice for excessive police violence, because of multiple mechanisms of qualified immunity.

All of these candid observations converge on the polarities of extreme exhaustion and wordless rage. The physical expression of their combination is "screaming outrage" and weeping. We choose to use the word "groaning" to stand for this collection of responses *in extrimis*. Groaning is the physical manifestation of the "pounding blows to our collective psyche."

An unstated but fundamental aspect of this outcry is the need for the presence of a witness to the plight of the groaner. Indeed, the sounds of such deep distress are calculated to attract such a witness. The functions of a witness are varied: companion, recorder, advocate, vicarious bearer, agent of relief. In a highly personal

11. Gladney, "A Devastating and Ruinous History," 37–38.

essay by novelist Jesmyn Ward, written in September 2020, the linkage between groaning and a witness is tight. It is important to set the context out of which this essay appeared.

In January 2020, Ward's husband and father of her children died of acute respiratory failure. She was awash in "hot wordless grief" at the same time the country was convulsed by the murder of George Floyd. In an essay she wrote while processing her own loss and grief, both in response to her husband's death and the death of George Floyd, she describes the uplifting power she experienced when she felt the presence of a witness to her groans.

> I woke to people in the streets. I woke to Minneapolis burning. I woke to protests in America's heartland, Black people blocking the highways. I woke to people doing the haka in New Zealand. I woke to hoodie-wearing teens, to John Boyega raising a fist in the air in London, even as he was afraid he would sink his career, but still, he raised his fist. I woke to droves of people, masses of people in Paris, sidewalk to sidewalk, moving like a river down the boulevards. I knew the Mississippi. I knew the plantations on its shores, the movement of enslaved and cotton up and down its eddies. The people marched, and I had never known that there could be rivers such as this, and as protesters chanted and stomped, as they grimaced and shouted and groaned, tears burned my eyes. They glazed my face.

It was in the viewing of the protestors all over the world that the power of a witness to suffering came to Ward.

> I sat in my stuffy pandemic bedroom and thought I might never stop crying. The revelation that Black Americans were not alone in this, that others around the world believed that Black Lives Matter broke something in me, some immutable belief I'd carried with me my whole life. . . . This is the belief that . . . Black lives have the same value as a plow horse or a grizzled donkey. I knew this. My family knew this. My people knew this, and we fought it, but we were convinced we would fight this reality alone. . . . I cried in wonder each time I saw protest around the

world because I recognized the people. I recognized the way they zip their hoodies, the way they raised their fists, the way they walked, the way they shouted. I recognized their action for what it was: witness. Even now, each day, they witness. . . . How revelatory that others witness our battles and stand up.[12]

As Ward vividly expresses, the witness to groaning exercises a transformative role in the contextualizing of groaning. This will become a major line of investigation in this book.

It is time now to begin to assess this collection of voices. It helps to begin by setting our assessment in some historical and behavioral context.

Initially, we should note that the sense of being exhausted and speechless did not arrive with the events of 2020. An important collection of essays, "Beyond Hate," is the cover story for November 12, 2018, *Time* magazine. It is keynoted by Nancy Gibbs, a former editor-in-chief at *Time* whose thoughts cast a long shadow forward over what we have been listening to.

Here then is the challenge: our normal responses aren't working. The spread of conspiracy theories as the "real truth" at least presumes that truth matters, even as the theories undermine it. Social networks designed to connect friends turn out to be expertly designed to create enemies. Fact-checking makes no difference; tribes trump truth. When reporters try to hold the [former] President [Donald J. Trump] accountable for inflaming the hatred, he attacks them for bias, for fueling division. When partisans on the left call for fighting fire with fire, they validate the tactics that debase our discourse.

Caught in the cross fire is a public not so much enraged as exhausted, at a loss to explain or escape the ugly, intellectually barren fever swamps that now pass for our public square. Conspiracy theories flourish as a substitute for the hard work of actual knowledge. They grant those who embrace them a shortcut to superiority: average people believe what they hear on the evening news or

12. Ward, "On Witness and Respair."

read in the papers, but you are smarter, you know better, you see the patterns and plots behind these events, the "globalists" pulling the strings, the "deep state" undermining your mission. You can't be fooled, you won't be puppets, you know better, you know the truth.

So what to do? The most eloquent politicians who warn of the toll this is taking are mainly the ones departing the scene. Where will we find moral leaders in an age of abdication, when "elites" of all kinds are suspect, whether teachers or preachers or scientists or scholars?[13]

I argue that the foregoing is not simply a collection of anecdotal comments but in fact bits of evidence of a cultural trauma gripping a fragmented and polarized social order whose complexity includes layers of Black racism, white superiority, and a social stupidity (Bonhoeffer) to what is required for a rich collective life. Cultural trauma is what emerges when "members of a collectivity feel they have been subjected to a horrendous event that leaves indelible marks upon their group consciousness, marking their memories forever and changing their future identity in fundamental and irreversible ways."[14] A chief impact on group consciousness is the damage to the bonds that attach people together, impairing their sense of community. The community no longer exists as an effective form of support to the self's worth.[15] A result of the shock of cultural trauma is to start a process of demanding "emotional, institutional, and symbolic reparation and reconstruction," which yields a new master narrative put to the service of restoring the self's identity.[16]

The purpose of this book is to direct readers to the master narrative of the crucified-resurrected Jesus, who is able to embrace exhausted, groaning persons and communities and renew moral vision, reinvigorate moral fiber, and return words of advocacy and praise to tongues that have been soured by profound hurt. Because

13. Gibbs, "The Only Way Forward," 23, italics added.

14. Dietrich, "Cultural Trauma," 148.

15. Boase, "The Traumatized Body," 194.

16. Holt, "Daughter Zion," 168–69.

of his solidarity on the cross with all who have been thrown into the abyss of abandonment, he, above all other figures, can be trusted. Because of his being raised from the dead, he brings a field of eschatological power to those whom the world has made to be nothing. Living within his cruciform presence, a way may and will be found out of no way.

At the conclusion we will draw from the insights gained to ask how the church might harness the power of groaning as it is christologically contextualized and transformed. We maintain that within the arena of the eschatological power held by the crucified Christ, groaning yields to a powerful witness to suffering and advocacy for its relief. Simply stated, this book offers encouragement and insight to pastoral leaders of congregations in their mission to provide renewal to exhausted and groaning persons by shaping a future in which they can thrive spiritually, even as they carry their scars.

Chapter 2

MAKING SENSE OF GROANING

B Y ITS VERY NATURE, groaning is sub-verbal. Elaine Scarry
observes in *The Body in Pain* that pain is language-shatter-
ing, causing a reversion to the pre-language of cries and groans.[1]
Dorothee Sölle notes how in deep suffering powerlessness and
speechlessness go together.[2] The study of deep trauma sheds light
on groaning. Bessel van der Kolk in his book *The Body Keeps the
Score* writes: "The memory of trauma is encoded in the viscera,
in heart-breaking and gut-wrenching emotions, in auto-immune
disorders and skeletal/muscular problems."[3] We can begin to understand groaning better if we place it in the study of emotions.

In his comprehensive study of the nature and function of emotions as "concern-based construals," Robert C. Roberts provides a
measurement of the intensity of an emotion as "a function of the
strength of the underlying concern, the vivacity of the construal,

1. Scarry, *The Body in Pain*, quoted by Miller, "Heaven's Prisoners," 17.

2. Sölle, *Suffering*, 71.

3. For an accessible review of this book, see Wilkinson, Review of *The
Body Keeps the Score*, 239–44. The quotation comes from p. 241. Eddie Glaude
speaks of how when he is thinking about Trumpism he must cope with "the
sourness that sits at the bottom of my stomach, and that, every now and again,
creeps up to the back of my throat. Bitter. Sour." See "The Magician's Serpent,"
9. Shelly Rambo, *Resurrecting Wounds*, 4, cites neurobiological studies pointing to "the limitations of language to articulating and bringing to light the
story of trauma."

and the rate of impingement of the construal on the concern."[4] Our examples offer very strong concerns of excessive police violence, systematic betrayal of trust, and dread for the future well-being of one's own life, as well as the lives of loved ones and community. These powerful impulses combine in our collective psyche to push at the boundaries of what is normal, rational life. Now, with the combination of (1) the crucial element of the horrific depiction of the death of George Floyd and (2) the deadly effects of a president speaking callous untruths, any state of normalcy or rationality is destroyed, and our response is vulnerable to being pushed to the level of guttural rage.[5]

However, even if incomprehensible sound is the only way the body can signal that the enormity of an experience outstrips the ability to put it into words, we should not conclude that the groaner is in a non-rational psychosomatic state. On the contrary, guided by Roberts's conception of emotion as conveying deeply felt concerns, these sub-verbal ejaculations are connected to intense *construals* about ourselves, our state of being. That is, there is a cognitive element within the non-sensical expression of exhaustion.[6] It is insightful to recall that Glaude found himself weeping as he "*thought* [my emphasis] about all the Black people who may watch the video in the middle of this pandemic and about the white people who would see it and ask the all-too-familiar questions about how do we change."

In the experience of groaning in frustration, dread, terror, or rage, I *see* myself as suffering, I *hate* the situation in which I am, I *conclude* something to be producing of rage.[7] All of the voices of groaning we have listened to are rooted in a settled construal about

---

4. Roberts, *Emotions*, 200. I am indebted to David J. Gouwens for introducing me to the fundamental work of Roberts.

5. See Roberts's careful taxonomy of the continuum of fear: anxiety, fright, dread, terror, panic, horror, and spook in *Emotions*, 198–202.

6 The use of non-sensical does not imply irrationality.

7. I am indebted to David J. Gouwens for pointing this out to me.

the circumstances in which the speakers find themselves. The emotion expressed discharges an identifiable burden of concern.[8]

This state-of-being, where a cognitive element becomes the burden of a non-sensical expression of rage, presents a challenge to how to cope effectively. We must look at this challenge carefully. Under the conditions of normality, a strong-willed person, as Roberts rightly affirms, ought to have the coping skills of perseverance, resoluteness, courage, patience, and self-control.[9] "Self-control can be among other things, a mastery of anger, resentment, malicious joy, scorn, hatred and envy."[10]

Anger, as we have seen, plays a major role in the rage we have been listening to. Anger, as Glaude pointed out, can be recognized as a signal that we know and understand real values (cognitive and propositional), and, under normal circumstances, anger can be contextualized by self-control so that the enraged person does not lose the ability to deliberate rationally.[11] Roberts suggests that an angry person could contextualize his anger through cognitive strategies, such as mental realignment, talking oneself into self-confidence, and confronting a challenge straight-on with a show of imagined strength. He writes, "The self-controlled person cannot manage adverse emotions and impulses without effective resources for dispelling, mitigating, and shaping them."[12]

However, someone who reels in screaming outrage from the "pounding blows to our collective psyche" might not be helped by only these cognitive strategies. We have listened to the voicing of wrongs that strike at the gut level and bring gut-wrenching anger/

---

8. Roberts, "Emotions among the Virtues" and "Emotions as Access." Roberts focuses on five chief emotions—joy, gratitude, contrition, hope, and peace—that give epistemic access to central truths of Christian faith. See his *Spiritual Emotions*, 11–13. In his analysis of the relation of emotions and feelings, Roberts describes criteria for the truth of feelings as well. See *Emotions: An Essay*. For an accessible introduction to research supporting the cognitive element in emotion, see Levine, *Healing the Reason-Emotion Split*.

9. Roberts, "Will Power."

10. Roberts, "Will Power," 245.

11. Roberts, *Emotions in the Moral Life*, 29–31.

12. Roberts, "Emotions among the Virtues," 58.

rage. The suffering one may not be able, in understandable words, to plumb the depths of what it is that grips those in traumatizing situations. As Eddie Glaude explains:

> Anger and fear make a combustible mixture. More than 140 cities have exploded since Floyd's death. Pundits and politicians have denounced the violence. Police have responded with violence of their own. . . . Contempt, spite, and insult are felt in every encounter.
>
> The anger results from accumulated grievance. George Floyd is just among the latest in a long list of our dead at the hands of police. . . . This kind of expression of anger is never just about the single incident; it carries with it every moment in which the society has told people they are disposable. The horrors of the auction block, the brutality of the lynching tree, the back-breaking work of the cotton field and the slaughterhouses, the sounds of clanging chains on the chain gang, and the daily disregard fuel the rage.[13]

What, then, is the propositional content of groaning?[14] *It goes beyond being rational, but the groaner is definitely not irrational.* Therefore, if trauma is to be healed, groaning must be contextualized some way that includes more than the rational.

This insight should make us, following Glaude, wary of writing off the groaner as someone who has simply lost the capacity to be self-controlled or self-managed. In fact, the groaner may be laboring under such a vast burden that it cannot be controlled or managed. Assuming that one who is speechless or can only emit

13. Glaude, "We Cannot Wait," 24. O'Connor in her interpretation of Lamentations sketches "the cycle of collapse of meaning leading to despair leading to anger, leading to violence." She cites Cornell West's observation of "nihilism" and the "murky waters of dread and despair that now flood the streets of black America, . . . the monumental eclipse of hope, the unprecedented crisis of meaning, the incredible disregard for human (especially black) life and property." *Lamentations*, 90–91. The citation is from West, *Race Matters*, 19.

14. Roberts, *Emotions: An Essay*, 320, says that the "adult feeler of the emotion will identify it by its grammatical features, that is, by the types of its propositional content, including the actions, if any, that he is inclined to perform in consequence of seeing the situation as he does."

non-sensical sounds has "lost it" actually denigrates the weightiness of the burden of truth such behavior expresses.[15] So, not only is the personhood of the groaner devalued as a supposedly deficient person, as someone who lacks the abilities to cope with life's trials, but the deep truth of groaning is discounted.[16]

Moreover, relying only on cognitive strategies as a means of restoring one's self-control runs afoul of evidence that argues that the burden of concern conveyed by groaning cannot be plumbed and engaged simply rationally.[17] We cannot talk ourselves out of exhaustion and rage. Studies of the effects of trauma point out that when we are traumatized, the left logical brain shuts down, "leaving the ability to tell a story to the right brain—a function it cannot and won't handle."[18] Simply put, our rational brain cannot talk our emotional brain out of the reality in which it is entrapped. Unfortunately, all too often when the freight of our concerns reflected in groaning cannot be discharged through rational thought, a frequent recourse is to off-load it by engaging in extreme actions, sometimes harmful or violent, as exemplified by the actions of members of both extreme right-wing and left-wing groups. It is critical, therefore, that strategies be fashioned that have the ability to reach into what is being communicated through the emotion

15. See Roberts, *Emotions: An Essay*, for a discussion of the seven criteria for truth in feelings. His exposition of the criteria "situational fit" and "survival of reflection" are especially relevant to the present discussion.

16. Roberts, *The Strengths*, 113–14, may not have recognized this possibility when he writes, "If we lack self-control, patience, and perseverance, it is because we have not practiced these things. It is a failure for which we can be called to account, whatever may be the environmental factors that encourage it." I would ask: Does this mean that the groaning is *our* fault? While this may be true for the majority of experience, our investigation centers on the extremity where one is no longer able to follow Roberts's advice to "take strategic advantage of memory, imagination, the power of conceptualize, to tease out of yourself" impulses of joy, hope, contrition, gratitude and peace to contextualize the burden of groaning (*Strengths*, 115).

17. This is confirmed by studies in the treatment of deep trauma. For accessible surveys, see Brooks, "Mental Health," and Sengal, "On Endless Loop."

18. Viveiros, review of *The Body Keeps the Score*, 167.

of groaning and actions envisioned that have maximum effect of reordering one's circumstances.

Roberts asserts, "I submit that joy, hope, contrition, gratitude and peace function, for the Christian, as such resources."[19] In what follows, I hope to build on his claim that such a Christian framework has the ability to reach into what is being communicated through the emotion of groaning. Such a Christian framework provides a home in which the profound bruising that issues in groaning will be recognized in terms of its spiritual costs and from the resource of the Christian Bible a pathway to restoration be discerned.

The first-person accounts we have listened to take in a wide swath of speakers. Each, in their own way, carries the human cost of being a victim of white supremacy, or a victim of systemic lying, or a victim of cultural betrayal. The range of voices we have heard describes an arc of groaning that registers a loss of humanity to everyone. Yet, there is also an important spiritual cost that must be reckoned with. This, in my judgment, gives to groaning its most searing quality. The spiritual cost is rooted in the collapse of a structure of meaning based on theological convictions. This is the point of engagement of our investigation.

Groaning comes out of a spiritual crisis where one has lost control of one's self because the structure of meaning which has functioned to make sense of one's self has collapsed. The American Black theologian James H. Evans Jr. cites with approval how a South African theologian, Manas Buthelezi, puts the propositional content of groaning:

> Out of this mental and emotional torture arise a number
> of existential questions, "After all, who am I?" "What is
> the destiny of my being and mode of existence?" "How
> can I so live as to overcome what militates against the
> realization of my destiny as a human being?" . . . "Can
> I realize my authentic humanity in the medium of my
> blackness?" "Is my blackness some fatalistic road block

19. Roberts, "Emotions among the Virtues," 58.

to life or a context within which God has made it possible for me to be an authentic man?"[20]

These questions cannot be chalked up to the self's not being
able to control feelings and limit a temptation to fall away from
trust in God. The groaner indicates the loss of something spiritual
that is critically important in supporting sanity and verbality. An
audible emotion (1) indicates spiritual costs associated with the
loss of the structure of meaning, (2) conveys the burden of that
cost, and (3) by means of this emotion affirms that what is lost actually exists. The groaner vigorously advocates for the restoration
of a lost structure of meaning and may even name the source from
whence that restoration is expected to originate. Even if the groaning is non-sensical, its object is the explication of the spiritual
costs tied to the loss of a structure of meaning and an appeal for
its restoration. The emotion of groaning is to convey the burden
of a spiritual cost. As such, groaning is something more than the
physiological registering of that emotion.[21]

This study is undertaken on the foundation that any release
from the bonds of groaning will proceed from the claims of the
lordship of a crucified-resurrected Jesus. By means of the wrenching cry of the crucified Jesus (Mark 15:37) God joins in solidarity
with all who find themselves transfixed in screaming rage. In a
later chapter we describe how both testaments converge on the
point of the cross of Jesus. On the cross, God collapses the distance between the abandoning God and the one who is groaning.
The astonishing and provocative message at the heart of Christian
faith is that God's utter identification with the extremes of human
suffering is so that God's victory, in resurrecting Jesus, over all that
reduces humans to groaning catches up with new life all persons
who have been pummeled.

20. Buthelezi, "The Theological Meaning of True Humanity," 93, quoted by
Evans, We Have Been Believers, 133.

21. Roberts calls such physiological manifestations "the feelings of construed condition, or feelings of self-estimate." See "What an Emotion Is," 185,
187–88.

God makes the very circumstances designed to grind humans down into submission become the context for experiencing the very thing they were designed to subvert. God radically identifies with the human and spiritual cost of devaluing in order to redeem humanity. Thus God proves that God is ultimately reliable, and that humans can take hope, even in darkest despair and screaming rage, that God's intentions for humanity will prevail. This is the cruciform resetting of the circumstances.[22]

Such an approach offers the church several openings in pastorally relating to people who are in the grip of groaning. First, pastors can assure them that their voices, however inarticulate, carry integrity and reality. Their groaning is an authentic meeting place for them and God. In that meeting, God is attentive to their groans, and they are affirmed as competent actors.

Second, the church can engage trauma at its deepest level with effectiveness and authenticity through the power of worship. Raging anger can be contextualized through the liturgy, at the sensory level of reception. That is, the hurts, the dashed hopes, the dread, the rage of our collective psyche can be ventilated and embraced in the mysterious rendering through worship of the crucified-resurrected Jesus.

In particular, the testimony from the Black church will confirm the power of song and spoken word and movement to grapple with deep hurt and trauma in order to free the damaged person to renewed engagement with the powers of white supremacy.

Roberts writes of such a rendering that it "envelopes you like an atmosphere, comes down on you and grabs you almost without your consent." Contributing to this "atmosphere" are "people of course, but the language of faith, the hymns, the windows and shades of light and darkness in the sanctuary, the smells."[23] He sees the need for a psychic moment wherein a suffering one recognizes that her most inarticulate rage is embraced by the crucified Jesus who brings her into his power field of stamina and freedom. In

22. I have explored this topic in *Aliens in Your Native Land*. For the concept of resetting, see also, Roberts, "Emotions among the Virtues," 56.

23. Roberts, *The Strengths of a Christian*, 20.

such moments one sees with the heart and experiences being touched in one's deepest recess of feeling.[24]

In sum, in coming into this communion with the crucified Jesus, the worshipper also brushes up against the field of eschatological power in the resurrected Jesus. Within the field of this power one becomes aware of new possibilities, resulting in spiritual renewal, even to someone who persists in rage, and bringing the promise of a redirection of the energy of that rage into visions of life and for its flourishing.

24. Roberts, *The Strength of a Christian*, 40–42.

Chapter 3

GROANING IN LAMENTATIONS 1
Sounds in Search of a Witness

T HE IMPACT OF EXTREME SITUATIONS of distress that issue in
groaning, such as those we have documented, can sensitize
the biblical interpreter to the presence of situations in biblical
texts where the burden of concern exceeds the ability of words
to convey, leaving the utterance of groans the only choice to discharge that burden.[1] One does not have to go far in searching for
examples before confronting the massive outpouring of groaning in
Lamentations. The discussion in this chapter and the following one
explores how suffering under the current state of racial aggression
calls out to readers of Scripture to see extreme suffering of any kind
in the context of the suffering of Lamentations, in other words, "to
read the tears of the world through the tears of Lamentations and
vice versa."[2]

It is perhaps ironic that in the Bible's many words there are
texts referencing instances where words run out, where words are
not adequate to carry the burden of concern, and sounds are all
that remain. This is what we are calling "groaning." While texts in

1. Boase, "The Traumatized Body," 196, calls this the "language of inar-
ticulateness in which pain and suffering are represented through audible but
nonverbal language."

2. Parry, "Prolegomena," 410. See also, O'Connor, *Lamentations.*

the Hebrew Bible that include the word for groaning (אנה/ 'nh) are found in the major prophets and the book of Psalms, Lamentations 1 uses this word five times in its twenty-two verses, (4, 8, 11, 21, 22), making it the highest concentration of the experience of running out of words found in the Old Testament. In a major commentary on Lamentations, Renkema comments: "[Groaning] does not lend itself to everyday use; it is primarily found, rather, in the context of existential distress brought on by oppression (Exod 2:23), godless tyranny (Prov 29:2), serious illness (Pss 6:7, 102:6), or labor pains (Jer 11:12). Wherever it is found, it gives expression to the strenuous and wearisome as well as the visible and audible nature of such groans."[3] Lamentations 1 is important to study because it shows both the breadth of the situations causing groaning as well as the complexity of the concern carried by the emotion. The text is also notable for stating what is needed, but lacking in Lamentations, to begin a response that would be transformative of what this emotion conveys.

In the Bible, groaning may be found within the genre of the lament as an intense form of calling out to God. O'Connor defines the genre: "Laments are prayers that erupt from wounds, burst out of unbearable pain, and bring it to language. Laments complain, shout, and protest. They take anger and despair before God and the community. They are acts of fidelity. In vulnerability and honesty, they cling obstinately to God and demand for God to see, hear, and act."[4] The poems of Lamentations are lament-like in form with elements of the form occurring throughout the book.

---

3. Renkema, *Lamentations*, 115.

4. O'Connor, *Lamentations*, 8. See also the description of Claus Westermann: "Even at its lowest moments the nation experienced its own history as a context that had meaning—or at least ought to have meaning. It took on meaning in that God was at work in it. Yet the nation experienced the plight it was in as an absurdity that confronted God with the question, 'Why?' How can God bring such profound suffering upon people—if indeed they are his people—when he has previously done such great things for them? Insofar as the absurd is laid before God, the lament of the nation contains a dimension of protest, the protest of a people who cannot understand what has happened or has been done to them." *Praise and Lament*, 270–71.

The Bible also testifies to a God who is attentive to inarticulate groans. Walter Brueggemann states the relationship between boldly speaking our hurt and the God who is attentive:

> In this moment of communication about hurt, we are close to the central oddity of the Old Testament. That oddity occurs in two parts. On the one hand, this community has a bold voice for hurt. It is prepared to take the risk and subvert the settled world because of its hurt. Israel will speak. On the other hand, this God has an attentive ear for hurt. Yahweh is now implicated irreversibly in Israel's hurt. God is bonded to Israel around the quintessential human reality of hurt. The God of Israel will never again be unhurt or unaware of Israel's hurt. God takes the hurt of earth into God's own life and heaven is thereby transformed. The hurt, noticed and voiced, becomes the peculiar mode of linking earth to heaven, Israel to Yahweh.[5]

The entirety of Lamentations explores this relationship between boldly speaking our hurt and the God who is, and is not, attentive.

The questions of dating, authorship, and setting are carefully described in major commentaries.[6] The general consensus is that Lamentations was written sometime after the fall of Jerusalem and destruction of the temple on Mount Zion by Babylonian forces in the first quarter of the sixth century. The poems in its five chapters are structured, more or less, according to an alphabetic acrostic model where the first verse begins with the first letter of the Hebrew alphabet and following verses begin with successive letters until the alphabet is completed.

As befits its name and setting, Lamentations preserves the collective response to devastating trauma involving tremendous loss of life, unspeakable cruelty, catastrophic material destruction, dire humanitarian threats, and widespread scrambling of

---

5. Brueggemann, "The Rhetoric of Hurt and Hope," 73.

6. O'Connor, *Lamentations*; Linafelt, *Surviving Lamentations*; Parry, *Lamentations*.

the spatial, spiritual, and ideological foundations supporting existential meaning. Our use of the term *trauma* concentrates on its manifestation in cultural settings. This is in contrast to investigating records of a psychoanalytic understanding of trauma in an individual, which are unavailable to the student of the ancient Near East. Jan Dietrich finds helpful Jeffrey Alexander's identification that "cultural trauma occurs when members of a collectivity *feel* they have been subjected to a horrendous event that leaves indelible marks upon their group consciousness, marking their memories forever and changing their future identity in fundamental and irrevocable ways."[7] Dietrich adds to this definition another important aspect: the very *incomprehensibility* of the events overwhelms humans and drives them to attempt various interpretive strategies, such as "hiding, explaining away, rationalizing or in other ways domesticating or neutralizing the occurrences which objectively, potentially, may be traumatizing."[8] Records of such behavior are available to the student of the ancient Near East, and Lamentations exemplifies how Israel confronted the very incomprehensibility of their Babylonian exile. Kathleen M. O'Connor underscores that, "to the extent that biblical texts address wounds of traumatic violence, they do so in non-medical ways, through artistic and intuitive literary approaches, using resources already available in the culture."[9]

The acrostically structured poetry of Lamentations strongly suggests that the poems intend to probe the depth of suffering "from A to Z." The discipline of writing each verse this way creates a certain amount of overlapping and doubling back of the content, having the effect of layering upon the reader the enormity of the suffering, and the polyphonic approach ventures toward making sense out of incomprehensibility.

Elise K. Holt comments that it is significant that the period when Lamentations was being formed coincides "with the general commencement of the writing down of the Old Testament books

---

7. Dietrich, "Cultural Traumas," 148, citing Alexander, *Cultural Trauma*, 1.

8. Dietrich, "Cultural Traumas," 149.

9. O'Connor, "How Trauma Studies," 211.

in the so-called axial age. . . . Writing and literacy is the implied prerequisite for the very form of Lamentations, the alphabetic acrostic."[10] She draws an important conclusion from this circumstance. "The theological discussions we encounter in the books of Jeremiah and Lamentations are thus parts of the theoretical culture of the axial age, the period so labeled by Karl Jaspers, indicating a period of cultural transformations in the first millennium BCE of many antique societies. . . . Indeed, the criticism of what Walter Brueggemann has labeled 'common theology' presupposes the theoretical culture of the axial age."[11]

I will argue that the placement of references to groaning within Lamentations 1 gives to the poem a certain unity that ties together the content of the poem, which, because of its overlapping nature, may appear, at first reading, to be disjointed. These references to groaning occur in vv. 4, 8, 11, 21, and 22. Physiological descriptions of groaning occur in vv. 2, 16, and 20. Verse 11 is the midpoint of the poem and vv. 21 and 22 conclude the poem.

I argue further that groaning provides a hermeneutical guide to this poem and to those that follow. What emerges is an organization of the poem into four sets of four verses with each set ending in groaning except the third set where groaning is moved from the fourth verse (12) to the midpoint (11). Furthermore, I will argue that the verses in which groaning is mentioned act like a "pressure valve," a tipping point, releasing the depth of pain to which the preceding verses in the set have been building.[12] Kathleen O'Connor, drawing on the work of poets Jane Cooper and R. T. Gaughan, points out that Lamentations "gives words and

10. Holt, "Daughter Zion," 169–71.

11. Holt, "Daughter Zion," 170. Holt is referencing Jaspers, *The Origin and Goal of History.* "Common theology" indicates a theology common to all ancient Near Eastern communities that legitimizes political and religious structures. See Brueggemann, *Theology,* 5–15.

12. This has not been recognized, so far as I can tell, by commentators. Renkema, *Lamentations,* 171, however, comments at Lamentations 1:16 that the phrase "for these things" "should be seen as causal. It refers back to the content of the complaints daughter Zion has expressed . . . and to which the present strophe alludes in an abridge[d] fashion."

shape to inchoate and unspeakable experiences; it provides suffering's 'necessary echo' from outside the experience, and it reveals
survivors' fierce graspings for life in ways readers recognize to be
true. Lamentations is an echo chamber and a hall of mirrors."[13]
This pattern exhausts itself at the conclusion of the poem, where
"groaning" appears twice in vv. 21–22 in conjunction with the central theological problem of Lamentations. I define this problem by
how the poem depicts God as the anti-shepherd of Israel and I
will discuss this metaphor by relating Lamentations 1 to Psalm 23
in the next chapter. The following analysis will demonstrate my
proposals.

Lamentations 1:1–4

How lonely sits the city[14]
that once was full of people!
How like a widow she has become,
she that was great among the
    nations!
She that was a princess among the
    provinces
has become a vassal.
[2] She weeps bitterly in the night,
with tears on her cheeks;
among all her lovers
she has no one to comfort her;
all her friends have dealt treacher-
    ously with her,
they have become her enemies.

[3] Judah has gone into exile with
    suffering
and hard servitude;
she lives now among the nations,
and finds no resting place;
her pursuers have all overtaken her
in the midst of her distress.
[4] The roads to Zion mourn,
for no one comes to the festivals;
all her gates are desolate,
her priests groan;
her young girls grieve,
and her lot is bitter,

13. O'Connor, *Lamentations*, 103.

14. The poet uses interchangeably a set of words to stand for defeated and
exiled Israel/Judah: Zion, Jerusalem, city, widowed mother/daughter. While
certain aspects are emphasized by the choice of word, this does not impinge on
our investigation of groaning. Maier, "Body Space as Public Space," 126, elaborates: "The female personification of Jerusalem is based on the idea that a city
provides food and shelter for its inhabitants—like a mother for her children.
In most biblical texts that personify the city the roles of mother, daughter, and
wife are intertwined. Such a literary intensification aims at establishing an exclusive relationship between God and the city."

The poem begins with a sympathetic narrator confronting the reader with the massive devastation and isolation of the nation of Israel, personified in the collective symbol of Zion as a bereft mother and disgraced supplicant.[15] This trauma causes groaning, registered by unrelieved weeping. She has no comforter, a personage typically linked with groaning (v. 22), because she has been betrayed by her "friends," a reference to nations with whom she was once in alliances. Exiled to a life of suffering, hard labor, constant removal, and persistent harrowing has the effect of hollowing the land of Israel of its native born. The poem makes the daring move where this compounded human suffering leaps to fasten upon the infrastructure, the roads and gates, that supported the center of Zion's character, the temple: "At the hands of the poet the inanimate routes to Zion come alive and lament the death of worship. The roads mourn and the gates are desolate. . . . The loss is so great that the *very architecture* of Zion joins in with her inhabitants to lament."[16]

The magnitude of these losses is indicative of why it is beyond the ability of words to express fully, leaving groaning the only option for the priests of Zion to discharge the pressure of what this loss implies. Since Israel's relationship with God was lived out through the cult, the implications of its loss created the terrifying possibility that God would no longer be their comforter, something for which priests had no language to handle, only groaning.

15. See the commentaries for discussion of the varied roles the narrator and Zion play in voicing the content of this chapter.

16. Parry, *Lamentations*, 47. See the similar expression of Zion as woman and architectural lament in Isa 3:26: "And her gates shall lament and mourn; ravaged, she shall sit upon the ground."

Lamentations 1:5–8

⁵ Her foes have become the masters,
her enemies prosper,
because the LORD has made her
  suffer
for the multitude of her
  transgressions;
her children have gone away,
captives before the foe.
⁶ From daughter Zion has departed
all her majesty.
Her princes have become like stags
that find no pasture;
they fled without strength
before the pursuer.

⁷ Jerusalem remembers,
in the days of her affliction and
  wandering,
all the precious things
that were hers in days of old.
When her people fell into the hand
  of the foe,
and there was no one to help her,
the foe looked on mocking
over her downfall.
⁸ Jerusalem sinned grievously,
so she has become a mockery;
all who honored her despise her,
for they have seen her nakedness;
she herself groans,
and turns her face away.

The poem continues with the narrator providing a catalogue of one loss heaped upon another: a reversal of status to vassalage, the taking away of children (her future) by oppressors, the stripping of majesty pointed up by the imagery of the ignominious flight of nobility (compare v. 3c), the haunting memory of former grandeur, which still gnaws, compounded by the betrayal by allies all leave her helpless. But the full realization of her loss will not come from such large-scale events. It will come from the look of mocking on the faces of Zion's foes as they subject her to the cruelties of objectification and shame. She is rendered as something worthless as she is publicly humiliated by being stripped so that her naked body would be exposed for all to stare at.[17] This is so utterly shaming that she is driven beyond words to speak of her humiliation. The accumulated weight of her shame can only be

---

17. Parry, "Lamentations and the Poetic Politics of Prayer," 68, comments: "Lamentations . . . bears witness to the trauma created by imperial strategies designed to break the will of a stubborn vassal state. [These strategies] cripple and humiliate the rebel state as a lesson to its citizens and to others who might be tempted to rebel. This was the imperial politics of violence and we would do well to view Lamentations as a reaction to 'state-sponsored terrorism.'"

vented through groaning and averting her gaze from the leering onlookers.[18]

In this second set occurs for the first time an issue that cannot be avoided when the collapse of a structure of meaning of this magnitude occurs: the relationship between cause and event, between sin and suffering. The set begins and ends with a judgment, perhaps spoken by an outside observer,[19] which puts the cause of the suffering of Jerusalem/Zion squarely to Yahweh's punishing her for her sin. It is reasonable to assume that Jerusalem/Zion shares in that understanding, which adds to her suffering such a depth that outstrips any words she might use for a confession. This load can only be discharged through groaning. The operative track is that sin causes punishment, which creates humiliation issuing in groaning. Acknowledgment of sin functions to potentiate the groaning.[20] Each subsequent set of four verses will contain a version of the relationship of sin to suffering. The final two verses of the poem will use two occurrences of groaning in collaboration with the explanation of suffering to state the theological problem of Lamentations. Later in this chapter we will attempt to summarize Lamentations' complex relating of sin to suffering.

18. Parry, "The Ethics of Lament," 146. See the helpful discussion of alternative understandings of Jerusalem's nakedness in Parry, *Lamentations*, 50–53.

19. O'Connor, *Lamentations*, and Allen, *Liturgy of Grief*, provide helpful discussions of the identity and function of the narrator.

20. Parry, "The Ethics of Lament," 146, provides balanced comment: "It is the narrator alone who speaks of Zion as disgraced by being stripped naked and raped (1:8b, 10). . . . Zion herself is so humiliated that she just groans and averts her gaze from the onlookers (1:8c). She cannot bring herself to speak of her humiliation in such terms. But it is not clear that by speaking of her humiliation this way he accentuates her sins so much as nuances them differently."

Lamentations 1:9–12

⁹ Her uncleanness was in her skirts; / she took no thought of her future; / her downfall was appalling, / with none to comfort her.	¹¹ All her people groan / as they search for bread; / they trade their treasures for food / to revive their strength.
"O Lord, look at my affliction, / for the enemy has triumphed!" / ¹⁰ Enemies have stretched out their hands / over all her precious things; / she has even seen the nations / invade her sanctuary, / those whom you forbade / to enter your congregation.	Look, O Lord, and see / how worthless I have become. / ¹² Is it nothing to you, all you who pass by? / Look and see / if there is any sorrow like my sorrow, / which was brought upon me, / which the Lord inflicted / on the day of his fierce anger.

The likelihood that "groaning" plays an architectural role in Lamentations 1 is enhanced by its placement in v. 11, which is the midpoint of the twenty-two-verse lament. This occurrence of groaning takes the voices of groaners from priests (v. 4) to Jerusalem (v. 8) and amplifies them to the entire populace.

The movement of groaning from the last verse in the four-verse set to the midpoint of the poem calls for a special analysis of this four-verse set. While the verses of this set are each constructed as a series of three bicola, the display above shows that they may scan differently, as might befit being at the heart of the poem, so to link several major themes.

We propose a parallel development of alternating sections, two bicola followed by four bicola. In the two bicola sections (vv. 9ab and 11ab) the narrator painfully describes appalling suffering of Zion (v. 9) and her people (v. 11). Verse 9b connects this suffering with the lack of a comforter, and v. 11b links suffering to a second theme, the desperate search to revive strength (literally "to revive soul").

These two themes, *no comforter* and *reviving soul*, are present throughout the poem. The "comforter" occurs in vv. 2, 3 (in the nominative form "resting place"), 9, 16, 17, and 21, where it is paired with groaning. "Restoring soul" is used in v. 11 in the context of groaning, and vv. 16 and 19. Lamentations 1:16 places these two ideas in direct parallelism: "for a comforter is far from me,/ one to revive my courage" (literally "my soul"). Here the doubling of *no help* triggers such a crisis that it forces the eruption of a graphic physiological demonstration of groaning.

The parallel sets of two bicola, 9ab and 11ab, are each followed by parallel sets of four bicola. They reproduce direct speech by Zion and have the effect of interrupting the narrator's speech with urgent pleas.[21] While each of these sets has unique features, they are strikingly similar. Both open by addressing Yahweh which marks the first occasion in the book of such address. This is urgent speech with the command for Yahweh to pay attention and see Zion's profound crisis.[22] The first set concentrates on the devastation of the enemy. The second set focuses on the pain Zion has suffered. These expanded sets surround the central v. 11ab, the bicola of groaning. We will now look at these four bicola sets more carefully.

In the first set (vv. 9c–10abc) we hear the horrors of the enemy from two speakers, Zion and the narrator. Zion speaks of her affliction as a direct result of the enemy's domination. The narrator identifies this affliction as the destruction of the temple. Graphic language is used to picture this destruction as a gang rape.[23] The impact of this sacrilege is far reaching. "Festivals and sabbaths are seasons of remembrance, points of contact between contingent time and mythic time, and hence assertions of cosmic order." In violating the sacred space "the symbolic links through which we situate ourselves in the world" are severed and life reverts to

21. For the relationship between these two speakers, see Miller, "Reading Voices," 397–400. Using the analysis of Mikhail Bakhtin, he calls this section "Active Double-Voiced Discourse." See Bakhtin, *Problems in Dostoevsky's Poetics.*

22. On the crucial necessity of the presence of a witness to suffering see O'Connor, *Lamentations*, 96–109. Boase points out that "in speaking, the woman resists the silence of trauma." "The Traumatized Body," 199.

23. Parry, *Lamentations*, 54, comments: "The sexual allusions are clear. The word 'enter' (בא/ *bā'*) is often used to describe the act of a man 'entering' a woman in sexual intercourse." In a footnote he gives further elaboration: "The word 'her precious things' (מחמדיה/*maḥdăêmaddhā*) can be used in a sexual context (Song 5:26: the woman's lover is 'altogether lovely')."

chaos.[24] A foreshadowing of this humiliating event has already been established in v. 4 with the mourning of the architecture of Zion and the ghostlike precincts of the temple, whose cumulative burden erupts in the groaning of the priests.

We have already noted that it is in this set that the poem makes its first direct address to Yahweh. "O LORD, look at my affliction, for the enemy has triumphed!" This is a plea for a witness to comfort and rescue; Yahweh's look is meant to counteract the leering of the enemy over Zion's naked shame (v. 8). This plea is intensified by an accusation against Yahweh's non-responsiveness to the enemy's bald transgression of Yahweh's explicit prohibition of foreigners entering the temple precincts. The accusing narrator quotes back to God Deuteronomy 23:3–6, "No Ammonite or Moabite shall be admitted to the assembly of the LORD," now applied broadly to other nations. This is an implicit criticism of God that God should allow such a shocking thing to happen; it is also a barb designed to motivate God to act to uphold divine honor by retaliating against those who have sullied God's wife/temple.[25] The fact that God does not respond to this attempt at persuasion adds weight to the possibility that God's absence is deliberate.

The precipitous devaluing of both lady Zion and God, her protector (vv. 9–10), is now matched by the devaluing of God's people, as described in v. 11ab. The people groan as they impoverish themselves materially in a desperate, futile search for sustenance. However, the groaning is not simply caused by a search for bread that comes up empty-handed. Attention to the context suggests that because this instance occurs at the midpoint it serves to gather up the tension that has been building from the start. The preceding sections of the poem have been preparing for this climax, beginning with the groaning that like a pressure valve discharges the burden of the priests of the raped temple (v. 4), followed by an expansion of the groaning to include the city that was shamefully

24. Landy, "Lamentations," 331.

25. Parry, "Lamentations and the Poetic Politics of Prayer," 71, and *Lamentations*, 54. Traditions of the inviolability of the temple can be found in the Prophets and Psalms; see, for example, Pss 46, 48, and 76.

abused (v. 8). The pattern of these two sets of four verses that end in groaning is now repeated with the third set of four verses where groaning is moved to the center verse (v. 11).

Here at the pivot verse of the acrostic, the poet situates groaning in its broadest manifestation, welling up from the general populace. The magnitude of this convulsion represents the cumulative pressure of the preceding groanings now combined with the descent into spiritual chaos due to the disgusting and debasing rape of the temple, the center upon which their lives were founded.[26] In sum, the groaning at v. 11ab conveys the speaker's confrontation at the most profound depths with the threat to life itself. There is no one to restore their soul.

Such catastrophic groaning can be compared with other descriptions of pandemic groaning, for example, the cry throughout Egypt at the effects of the death of the firstborn (Exod 11:6; 12:30), or of the panic that rippled through the army at the death of the Babylonian general Holofernes (Judith 14:19).

The second four-bicola set (11c–12abc) surrounding this cascading of groaning repeats Zion's shrill demand to look and see the worthlessness of God's people, just as the first set showed up the worthlessness of the temple/wife. Two respondents are addressed: God (v. 11c) and anyone within earshot (v. 12a). Each is implored to look and see. Sorrow without measure is the well-spring of inarticulate sounds. This cacophony is meant to attract the attention of any witness, especially God.

But it is not *irrational* noise. These two sets of extended commands "to look!" surround the outpouring of groaning in v. 11a with explicit statements of the burden of the concern. It is rather

---

26. Landy, "Lamentations," 330: "The same images repeat themselves at intervals, as if fixated in the memory, only to be carried ultimately to a logical inversion." Recall the collection of reactions to the death of George Floyd in the introduction which emphasize the repeatable nature of traumatizing memory. Shelly Rambo speaks of trauma as that which "does not get integrated in time and thus returns or remains, obstructing one's ability to engage the world as one did before." *Resurrecting Wounds*, 4.

that the magnitude of the burden requires sounds deeper than language to communicate that concern sufficiently.[27]

Excursus: Look and See! The Search for a Witness

The repetition of "look" and "see" underscores the imperative of God's taking notice, of being a witness, of being a mirror to such devastation.

"O Lord, look at my affliction, for the enemy has triumphed!" [10] Enemies have stretched out their hands over all her precious things; she has even seen the nations invade her sanctuary, those whom you forbade to enter your congregation.	Look, O Lord, and see how worthless I have become. [12] Is it nothing to you, all you who pass by? Look and see if there is any sorrow like my sorrow, which was brought upon me, which the Lord inflicted on the day of his fierce anger.

Who does look and see? The enemy looks and leers. The intensity attached to this question increases because the text does not record God's responding to the pleading. God is not the comforter, the restorer of soul. What God does is to make God's self present through the pain and sorrow afflicted in the power of God's fierce anger. This anger is God's answer to an observer's comment at the beginning of this set that Zion is culpable for sullying herself with foreign alliances without thinking about future consequences (as in v. 2).[28]

---

27. O'Conner, *Lamentations*, xiv: "Lamentations is about the collapse of a physical, emotional, and spiritual universe of an entire people, not about individual sorrows, except in a metaphoric and symbolic manner."

28. Some type of sexual transgression is probably indicated. In v. 2 Jerusalem's false lovers do not comfort her; they deal treacherously with her and become her enemies. Maier, "Body Space as Public Space," 126, observes: "Any relation of Zion's inhabitants to foreign nations or other gods would be called 'whoredom,' which is indeed the main accusation advanced by the prophets (Is 1:7; Jer 2–3, 13; Ezek 16:23.)." See O'Connor, *Lamentations*, 21–22, and Parry, *Lamentations*, 52–53.

However, the dominating imperative for the poet is not to explain suffering as punishment but to present suffering as going far beyond what any transgression could substantiate. The poet deliberately juxtaposes explanations of the calamity with descriptions of misery that must be addressed. This use of parataxis is not to establish connections between the opposites but to amplify the dissonances that shake previous understandings of morality.[29] In this set of four verses groaning does not reflect guilt so much as grievance.

The question of who does look and see remains open beyond the close of the first poem. Only in Lamentations 2 does an answer emerge, partial at best. When the second poem arrives, at its structural midpoint (2:11), groaning is described in its physiological manifestation:

> My eyes are spent with weeping;
> my stomach churns;
> my bile is poured out on the ground
> because of the destruction of my people,
> because infants and babes faint
> in the streets of the city.[30]

This is a scene of heart-rending terror, made further excruciating by the viscerally disturbing scene of v. 12:

---

29. Landy, "Lamentations," 330. Allan, *A Liturgy for Grief*, 20, catches this parataxis: "Lamentations comes across as a comprehensive mingling of nostalgic yearning, deep sadness, and angry protest with another item thrown into the mix, a sense of guilt." See also Tiemeyer, "The Doubtful Gain of Penitence," 110. "Turning to the Hebrew Bible, the lament psalms convey a *smorgasbord* of sufferers, ranging from those who suffer the punishment of their sins . . . to those who suffer because of no obvious fault of their own. . . . Indeed, a given psalm can contain both approaches (see Ps 69:5, 7–12 where the sufferer is aware of his sins, yet also laments that he suffers because of his actions for God's glory). There are examples where, from a human perspective, the divine punishment fits the crime and others where, again from our human perspective, the divine punishment appears to be excessive. Therefore, in line with the textual evidence cited above, penitential prayer and lament should not be pitted against each other, but each be given its due time and place."

30. See also Jer 4:19 and Job 30:27.

> They cry to their mothers,
> "Where is bread and wine?"
> as they faint like the wounded
> in the streets of the city,
> as their life is poured out
> on their mothers' bosom.

This trauma strikes a blow deep within the viscera of the lamenter (intestines in turmoil, liver poured out) which is telegraphed openly as copious weeping. The liver, in particular, was thought to be a highly sensitive organ. Hans Walter Wolf comments, "This is a way of describing measureless grief; in his sorrow the poet is no longer in control of his innermost feelings; his very life is poured out with his liver"[31] to correspond with the pouring out of life from the most defenseless.

Finally, there is one who sees and responds (2:13):

> What can I say for you, to what compare you,
> O daughter Jerusalem?
> To what can I liken you, that I may comfort you,
> O virgin daughter Zion?
> For vast as the sea is your ruin;
> who can heal you?

The speaker is someone, perhaps the narrator, who reflects back Zion's incomparable sorrow, sorrow that can be measured only by the vastness of the ocean, the silent unboundedness of the sea. This answer is partial, at best. Clearly, the speaker is not God. The narrator recognizes this and intensifies the renewal of this plea, "Look, O LORD, and consider! To whom have you done this? Should women eat their offspring, the children they have borne?" (2:20). O'Connor sets out the full dimensions of God's silence.

> The only possible answer that could fulfill Zion's cry would come from God. But God is silent. The only speaker who could proclaim light, hope, and a future in

---

31. Wolf, *Anthropology*, 64. Recall Eddie Glaude's comment referenced earlier that how when he is thinking about Trumpism he must cope with "the sourness that sits at the bottom of my stomach, and that, every now and again, creeps up to the back of my throat. Bitter . . . Sour."

these circumstances, is missing. God does not speak, respond, heal, see. When a people's symbolic narrative collapses, they "cannot move toward the future." They have neither plan nor rudder with which to guide their steps, claim their identity and provide safety. God's silence in Lamentations greatly exacerbates their suffering because it signifies the end of life as they have known it.[32]

To summarize our analysis up to this point: First, our discussion has established a crucial correspondence between the midpoints of Lamentations 1 and 2. Specific attention has been focused on the hermeneutical function of these midpoints to establish a perspective from which to read the book. The incremental buildup of the voices of groaning in Lamentations 1:4 and 8 issues in a crescendo of an unanswered question to God at the midpoint in Lamentations 1:11c. The creative arrangement in Lamentations 2:11–13 links the physiological manifestation of groaning (v. 11) to the narrator's answer that there is no-answer (v. 13) to the traumatizing blows of v. 12.

Second, the novel feature of the first poem is its division into sets of four verses that contain the word "groan" at or near the end of each set. However, the pattern of the first two sets is broken in the third one at the midpoint of the acrostic poem. Here the division of Lamentations 1:9–12 yields parallel sets of two bicola followed by four bicola. Because this breaks the strictly acrostic structure, it invites further reflection. Literary critic Francis Landry provides a helpful perspective:

> The acrostic provides a purely external structure for the poem, predictable and yet open to all the possibilities of expression and fragmentation. This assurance and freedom counteract the loss of political and religious structure described in the poem. They may be seen as an ironic wish-fulfilling gesture, an ineffectual assertion of control over language, and hence over thought, in the face of devastating reality. The acrostic is a sign of

32. O'Connor, *Lamentations*, 84–85.

language—the system of signs—in which all the letters of
the alphabet cooperate to generate meaning.[33]

We suggest that the breaking of the four bicola at 1:9–12 into
parallel sets of two and four, which (1) skillfully intertwines two
major themes of *no comforter* with *no revival of soul* and (2) surrounds the pandemic of groaning with demanding voices to "look
and see," is an instance of breaking the acrostic to signify how this
tight poetic form amounts to what Landry calls "an ineffectual assertion of control over language, and hence over thought, in the
face of devastating reality." God does not pick up the challenge to
rise to be the witness who comforts and restores the soul.[34]

In the next two sets of four verses the pattern will be capped
by a reference to the behavior of groaning.

Lamentations 1:13–16

[13] From on high he sent fire;
it went deep into my bones;
he spread a net for my feet;
he turned me back;
he has left me stunned,
faint all day long.
[14] My transgressions were bound
    into a yoke;
by his hand they were fastened
    together;
they weigh on my neck,
sapping my strength;
the Lord handed me over
to those whom I cannot withstand.

[15] The LORD has rejected
all my warriors in the midst of me;
he proclaimed a time against me
to crush my young men;
the Lord has trodden as in a wine
    press
the virgin daughter Judah.
[16] For these things I weep;
my eyes[35] flow with tears;
for a comforter is far from me,
one to revive my courage;
my children are desolate,
for the enemy has prevailed.

---

33. Landry, "Lamentations," 333.

34. To this point may be added what numerous critics have noticed regard-
ing the steady degradation of the acrostic structure spread over poems four
and five. See O'Connor, "Voices Arguing about Meaning," 29.

35. The underlying Masoretic text has "my eye, my eye." This repetition is
highly effective in communicating the unrelenting weeping of groaning. See
3:50, "My eyes will flow without ceasing, without respite, until the LORD from
heaven looks down and sees."

Far from being comforter and restorer of soul, Zion speaks of God as hostile warrior[36] who sends fire "deep into my bones,"[37] who places a yoke of sins to "weigh upon my neck," who determines to "crush my young men," and trample upon the innocence of "virgin daughter Judah," leaving Zion stunned and sapped in strength. Elizabeth Boase notes,

> Within Lamentations, divine absence and violent presence stand in contrast with each other, a contrast which creates tension in the text. . . . The presence of the Babylonians as the actual enemy is sidelined, with Yahweh portrayed as the enemy. Violent presence is a past experience of the divine, while the sense of divine absence is a present reality. The ongoing pain comes from divine absence in the wake of the active destruction.[38]

In this and the following set of four verses the word for groaning is not used, but its physiological affects are described in v. 16—deep and unremitting weeping, which we have encountered already in Lamentations 1:2 and 2:11. Terence Collins, who has studied the impact of such devastation on the physical body observes:

> Distressing, external circumstances produce a physiological reaction in a man [sic], which starts in his [sic] intestines and proceeds to affect his [sic] whole body, especially the heart. This physiological disturbance is actually a change in the physical composition of the inner organs, a general softening up, which initiates an outflow of the body's vital force. This outflow proceeds through the throat and eyes, and issues in the form of tears which are nothing less than the oozing out of the body's vital substance. The immediate consequence is that the subject is left weak and exhausted, in particular his [sic] eyes are considered to be wasting away through tears which

36. Parry, "Lamentations and the Poetic Politics of Prayer," 70.

37. Psalm 102:3–5 describes groaning in the context of the body's bones burning.

38. Boase, "Constructing Meaning," 466.

are part of their substance flowing out and sapping their strength.[39]

Verse 16 gathers up ("for these things") the burden of suffering caused by God the warrior: no comforter (vv. 2, 9), no restoring of soul (v. 11), the triumph of the enemy (v. 9). This burden is discharged in weeping, leaving the groaner weak with no comforter and no one to restore their soul (see v. 14c). This set makes clear that even though Mother Zion admits full culpability for the occurrence of her suffering, it is the experience of suffering under a strange and threatening God that is foregrounded.

Lamentations 1:17–20

[17] Zion stretches out her hands,
but there is no one to comfort her;
the LORD has commanded against Jacob
that his neighbors should become his foes;
Jerusalem has become
a filthy thing among them.
[18] The LORD is in the right,
for I have rebelled against his word;
but hear, all you peoples,
and behold my suffering;
my young women and young men
have gone into captivity.

[19] I called to my lovers
but they deceived me;
my priests and elders
perished in the city
while seeking food
to revive their strength.
[20] See, O LORD, how distressed I am;
my stomach churns,
my heart is wrung within me,
because I have been very rebellious.
In the street the sword bereaves;
in the house it is like death.

This final set of four verses is notable for its coda-like quality. In speeches by both the narrator and Zion the poet gathers up images that have been previously used to paint the excruciating picture of how a structure of meaning has collapsed for a people: the imploring for a witness (vv. 9, 11, 12), no comforter (vv. 2, 3 "resting place," 9, 16), turn-coat neighbors (vv. 2, 7), Jerusalem as a repulsive object (v. 9), the exile into captivity of the nation's future (vv. 3, 5), the decapitation of national leadership (vv. 6, 15), no restoring of soul (vv. 11, 16). Francis Landry comments, "The same

---

39. Collins "The Physiology of Tears," 18.

images repeat themselves at intervals, as if fixated in the memory, only to be carried ultimately to a logical inversion."[40] In both street and home, the places both public and private, where life should flourish, only death reigns.

The cumulative, screaming outrage from endless pounding blows to Zion's collective psyche erupts in a geyser of stomach bile and tears from a heart wrung dry (compare Lam 2:11). This disgusting scene is the physiological signature of groaning.

Compare Psalm 38:6–9:

> I am utterly bowed down and prostrate;
> all day long I go around mourning.
> For my loins are filled with burning,
> and there is no soundness in my flesh.
> I am utterly spent and crushed;
> I groan because of the tumult of my heart.
> O Lord, all my longing is known to you;
> my sighing is not hidden from you.

and Jeremiah 4:19:

> My bowels, my bowels! I writhe in pain!
> O, the walls of my heart! My heart is in turmoil! I cannot keep
> silent,
> For I hear the sound of the horn, the alarm of war!

In sum, this final set gathers up the four preceding sets of four verses, each set describing in a cascading fashion, aspects of Zion's degradation as a national people: isolation, becoming worthless, the absence of one who sees/comforts/restores soul, God as hostile warrior. Each set has been written to end with a statement of groaning or a vivid physiological description of groaning. The pool of groaning widens and deepens with each set.

In this final set, the path of the voicing of guilt and grievance takes a decided tilt toward the presentation of pain as pain.[41] "The

40. Landry, "Lamentations," 330. The emerging field of trauma-informed criticism of biblical texts suggests that this repetition of images is evidence of the survivors of trauma repeatedly and belatedly grappling with the experiences of extreme violence. See Yansen, *Daughter Zion's Trauma*, 5, 24.

41. Parry, *Lamentations*, 149. See also Thomas, "Lamentations and the Trustworthiness of God," 7.

Lord is in the right, for I have rebelled against his word; but hear, all you peoples, and behold my suffering." This may not finally satisfy some readers, however. What is the relationship between sinning against God and being punished? Lamentations, as we have been finding out, presents no simple answer but only a changing trajectory.

Linafelt calibrates this shift from a simple answer to a complex continuum: "Lamentations may be taken as an ancient example of survivor literature, a literature that is more about the expression of suffering than the meaning behind it, more about the contingencies of survival than the abstractions of sin and guilt, and more about protest as a religious posture than capitulation or confession."[42] Parry, however, may strike the best balance when he says: "Jerusalem, like the narrator, places more emphasis on her suffering than on her sin. The bulk of her words (1:9c, 11c, 12–16, 18–22) are designed to elicit pity and compassion for herself and her children."[43] She does not deny her sin, and she affirms that Yahweh as just and is justified in punishing her. However, her aim is salvation. "Zion draws attention to the presentation of pain rather than confession of guilt. . . . References to her transgressions are embedded in a general context the main focus of which is eliciting compassion for Zion."[44]

Looking back, the calculus between sin and pain in Lamentations 1 can be figured by the various voices of groaning in each of the four-verse sets. In the first set, groaning functioned to express the terror of being in isolation. In the second set, groaning issued forth out of Zion's abject shame from being dehumanized as a spoil of conquest as the consequence of punishment for innumerable transgressions. In the third set, groaning is separated from close relationship with sin. Groaning sits at the midpoint of the poem, surrounded by urgent, incessant pleas for attention to pain and sorrow, and underscored by noting the absence of a comforter/restorer. The mention of transgression occurs independently of this

42. Linafelt, "Surviving Lamentations (One More Time)," 62.

43. Parry, "The Ethics of Lament," 145.

44. Parry, "The Ethics of Lament," 149–50.

constellation and carries forward features of the preceding set of
the debased woman, now adding the suggestion of Zion's immoral
involvement in foreign alliances. In the fourth set, groaning was in
reaction to the transformation of God from anticipated comforter/
restorer to hostile warrior. Part of these hostile actions are the war-
rior-God binding transgressions as a yoke upon the neck of Zion,
suggesting that such a fixation on transgression indicates a change
in the character of God as a loving and gracious Lord. In the fifth
set, groaning bore the sum total of all the afflictions enumerated in
the poem. There is admission of guilt, but the emphasis falls upon
vectoring attention to the grievance of inordinate suffering.

This changing calculus between sin and suffering has roots in
the classic self-definition of God in Exodus 34:6–7:[45]

> [6] The Lord, the Lord,
> a God merciful and gracious,
> slow to anger,
> and abounding in steadfast love and faithfulness,
> [7] keeping steadfast love for the thousandth generation,
> forgiving iniquity and transgression and sin,
> yet by no means clearing the guilty,
> but visiting the iniquity of the parents
> upon the children
> and the children's children,
> to the third and the fourth generation.

The intensity of the pleas for relief from suffering is to motivate God to respond out of his graciousness at the sight of the
lamenter's recognition of the legitimacy of God's working from his
punitive aspects.[46] The implicit acknowledgment of the failure of

45. On the importance of this text for postexilic prophecy, see Bailey,
Living in the Language of God, 36–40.

46. While affirming with feminist criticism that the poem progressively
moves the attention of the reader to focus more on the presentation of the
pain of Zion as simply indiscriminate pain, the position articulated here keeps
the attention focused on the fact that only God can relieve that pain and does
not rely on Zion's maternal stature to mitigate her sin or motivate her relief.
See Mandolfo, "Dialogic Form Criticism," 87. In the following chapter I will
discuss this further.

the pleas to motivate is stated plainly in Lamentations 3:40–44: "Let us test and examine our ways. . . . We have transgressed and rebelled, but you have not forgiven. . . . You have wrapped yourself with a cloud so that no prayer can pass through."

Lamentations 1:21–22

²¹ They heard how I was groaning,
with no one to comfort me.
All my enemies heard of my
    trouble;
they are glad that you have done it.
Bring on the day you have
    announced,
and let them be as I am.
	²² Let all their evildoing come
	    before you;
	and deal with them
	as you have dealt with me
	because of all my transgressions;
	for my groans are many
	and my heart is faint.

The last two verses of the poem continue the pattern of reusing important elements of earlier verses but with significant advances in the message. Ongoing groaning begins and ends this set. There is no comforter and the heart is faint. The incessant cries for help throughout the poem have not been heeded by God. Anticipated restoring of soul has not occurred, which would have issued in glad praise. However, the enemies have heard the cries. They are glad for unremitting pain. So, while culpability for sin is not forgotten, confession seems pointless. Hence, the poem concludes not with a plea for help, but with a strong demand for vengeance. If God cannot or will not show mercy upon hearing Zion's admission of culpability, at least God can hurt Zion's enemies as much as God has hurt her.[47]

If the task of theodicy is "to justify God in the face of suffering,"[48] Lamentations 1 does not accomplish this. However, as we have seen, the existential struggle to explain suffering and evil

---

47. Notice the chiastic structure of v. 22, giving structure to this equivalency. Israel is testifying that their sin is not why they suffer so much. Nor is it the case that Israel believes God has withdrawn from them. They appeal to God's retributive justice.

48. See Boase, "Constructing Meaning in the Face of Suffering," 468.

and the intense tension between God and suffering is evident in the various voices that exist in competition with each other.

To review, we have described a strong presence of the motif of groaning in Lamentations 1 highlighting its strategic placement at regular intervals, at midpoint and at conclusion. This supports our contention that this specific reaction to the collapse of an entire structure of meaning provides the hermeneutical perspective for appreciating the book of Lamentations. It is noteworthy that "groaning" does not appear in any of the poems that follow, though the physiological manifestation of it through copious weeping and vomiting does (Lam 2:11; 3:48–49, 51). This might lend credence to the suggestion that Lamentations 1 was composed as an introduction to the collection, giving the reader a range of perspectives, a set of issues, from which to understand the collection as a whole. Thus, Lamentations 2:13 would be understood as an answer of the narrator to the pleas of Lamentations 1:9c; 11c, 12 to look and see! Lamentations 3:44 would be a definitive answer to God's unresponsiveness. The portrayal of God as warrior would be placed against the hopeful descriptions of divine aid in Lamentations 3:21–25 and 3:55–57. The ending of the book, Lamentations 5:21–22, picks up the motif of God as restorer in a last-ditch prayer whose hopes are severely choked by the final verse that underscores the remoteness of a silent God. "Restore us to yourself, O LORD, that we may be restored, renew our days as of old—unless you have utterly rejected us and are angry with us beyond measure" (Lam 5:21–22).[49] In sum, if Lamentations 1 asserts that groaning is all that is left to humans because words simply fail to convey the burden of concern, Lamentations 2–5 spell out events, feelings, and needs the impact of which lie deeper than words can tell.[50]

---

49. Other commentators translate the last part of this verse to follow the MT syntax of a protasis without an apodosis. "For if truly you have rejected us, raging bitterly against us—then . . . ." See Linafelt, "The Refusal of a Conclusion." We will utilize this option in the next chapter.

50. The question of whether Lamentations is a collection of separate poems that have been put together by a redactor or a unified composition is hotly debated. See Westermann, *Lamentations*, 58, 66–67, and Renkema, *Lamentations*, 36–40.

The primary theological and pastoral issue of the book is the absence of a witness who will take notice and make a way for mercy and relief to flow. In its place looms a God whose actions or lack thereof show persistent, implacable anger. In the next chapter we give this picture of God additional definition, after which we will marshal a canonical response aimed to respond to this picture.

Chapter 4

PSALM 23 AND LAMENTATIONS 1 IN CANONICAL INTERPRETATION

A looming issue generated by the poetry of Lamentations 1 is the lack of a divine response of relief and succor to the cries of groaning and the confession of transgression. Various attempts will be mounted in the course of Lamentations 2–5 to respond to this issue, ranging from gritty assurance to entertaining the unthinkable. For example, at the center point of chapter 3 there is the encouragement that "the Lord will not reject forever. Although he causes grief, he will have compassion according to the abundance of his steadfast love; for he does not willingly afflict or grieve anyone" (Lam 3:31–33, borrowing from Exod 34:6–7). The placement of this affirmation at the center point of the central chapter is proof of its use as a confessional marker. However, this is countered by the final words of the book: "Restore us to yourself, O Lord, that we may be restored, renew our days as of old—For if truly you have rejected us, raging bitterly against us—then . . ." (Lam 5:21–22).[1]

The power of the hermeneutical function of groaning in Lamentations 1 draws unto itself imagery that deepens the impression

1. This translation follows the MT syntax of a protasis without an apodosis. See Linafelt, "The Refusal of a Conclusion." Parry, *Lamentations*, 155, calls this fascinating and appealing but believes this is too modern for an ancient interpreter.

of God as unresponsive to pain and honesty. This part of the investigation concentrates on probable sources in Israel's literary bank upon which the poet drew to achieve the goal of foregrounding the unresponsive God.[2] At least two of those sources have already been identified. Commentators have recognized that at Lamentations 1:10 the accusing narrator quotes Deuteronomy 23:3–6 back to God: "No Ammonite or Moabite shall be admitted to the assembly of the LORD." This is now applied broadly to other nations. This is an implicit criticism of God that God should allow such a shocking thing to happen; it is also a barb designed to motivate God to act to uphold divine honor by retaliating against those who have sullied God's wife/temple. The fact that God does not respond to this pressure adds weight to the possibility that God's absence is deliberate.[3] A second text that provides grounding for the poet's wrestling with the calculus of pain and penitence is Exodus 34:6–7, which was considered in the previous chapter.

Another source for the content of Lamentations 1, which has not been given sufficient attention, is Psalm 23. For such a short psalm, it is astounding how profoundly it has shaped the content

2. Parry helpfully describes the "inner-biblical reuse of earlier traditions and texts in fresh ways to fit the changing context of the story. . . . The canon privileges certain texts . . . and invites unexpected readings that go beyond the 'original horizons' of the individual books—old stories are invited to be read against the expanding horizon of the grand story of God's relationship with his people as it moves ever onward." In "Prolegomena," 400.

3. Commentators cite *Lamentations Rabbah* XXIVii.1.I-2.C-D describing the following scene in heaven as evidence of later struggles with explaining the absence of God's defense of the temple: "At that moment the Holy One, blessed be he, wept, saying, 'Woe is me! What have I done! I have brought my Presence to dwell below on account of the Israelites, and now that they have sinned, I have gone back to my earlier dwelling. Heaven forefend that I now become a joke to the nations and an object of ridicule among the people.' . . . When the Holy One, blessed be he, saw the house of the sanctuary, he said, 'This is certainly my house, and this is my resting place, and the enemies have come and done whatever they pleased with it!' At that moment the Holy One, blessed be he, wept, saying, 'Woe is me for my house! O children of mine—where are you? O priests of mine—where are you? O you that love me—where are you? What shall I do for you? I warned you but you did not repent.'" See Parry, "The Trinity and Lament," 149.

of the poem of lament. The remainder of this discussion will make the case that Lamentations 1 is a type of anti-Psalm 23, drawing considerable imagery from that beloved psalm of trust to portray God as the anti-shepherd.[4] Psalm 23 thus becomes the template for grappling with the theological problem of God's absence.[5]

Only a few students of Lamentations have mentioned the poet's use of this psalm. In 1993 Jonathan D. Safren pointed to the similarity between נפשי ישובב "he restores my soul" in Psalm 23:3a to נפש להשיב "to revive their strength" in Lamentations 1:11 and נפשם את וישיבו "to keep alive" in Lamentations 1:19. In Lamentations 1:16 the absent comforter of Zion is described as "my reviver" נפשי משיב.[6]

In 2003 Van Hecke presented a careful study of the relationship between Psalm 23 and Lamentations 3:1–6, where he coined the word anti-Psalm 23. Referring to his essay in the course of our investigation will aid in understanding the distinctive use of the psalm in Lamentations 1. Van Hecke concludes:

> The authors of Lamentations deliberately conceptualized God as a bad shepherd or an anti-shepherd in Lam 3:1–6, and did so in direct (contrasting) reference to Ps 23. Not only do these verses of Lamentations call in mind some of the terminology of Ps 23, they also contain several reversed pastoral metaphors, serving as thematic links with the shepherd psalm.[7]

Based on his work, Claire-Antoinette Steiner in 2009 included a paragraph in her essay where she points to possible allusions in Lamentations 1 to the "psalm of the shepherd," which the poet uses in a critical way to deconstruct certain traditional

---

4. See Van Hecke, "Lamentations 3:1–6." See also Zechariah 11:4–17 as a type of anti-Psalm 23.

5. The emerging field of trauma-based interpretation of biblical texts points to the evidence of "theological dissonance or discord and deep psychological anguish" as signals of "the struggle intrinsic to testifying to experiences of trauma." See Yansen, *Daughter Zion's Trauma*, 2, 28.

6. Safren, "He Restoreth My Soul," 265–67.

7. Van Hecke, "Lamentations 3:1–6," 273.

images of God and to mount the poem's reproach to God who does not respond or attend to God's people.[8] These studies encourage additional work to gain greater appreciation of the influence Psalm 23 has made in formulating the poetry of Lamentations 1.

The enterprise of describing an author's alluding to another existing text involves the interpreter making decisions in the absence, many times, of the author's intention. Consequently, this requires the interpreter to exercise as much precision as possible in formulating the type of allusion suggested. Benjamin D. Sommer in his analysis of allusion in Isaiah 40–66 has provided a nomenclature for the various ways text-borrowing can happen.[9]

> An *allusion* in a text to an earlier one modifies the meaning of the later text, while an *echo* merely reuses a phrase found in an earlier text without modifying the meaning of either. *Exegesis* is understood as a later attempt to clarify the meaning of the earlier text. An exegetical text cannot exist without the former. In contrast, a *revision* of an earlier text seeks to replace the earlier text. Similarly, a *polemic* text attempts to take the place of the earlier text but, at the same time, depends on the older text whilst rejecting it.

Sommer's nomenclature complements Mikhail Bakhtin's dialogic linguistics. "Every utterance must be regarded primarily as a response to preceding utterances of the given sphere. . . . Each utterance refutes, affirms, supplements, and relies on the others, presupposes them to be known, and somehow takes them into account. . . . It is impossible to determine its position without correlating it with other positions."[10] We will attend to the double-voiced character of Lamentations 1 after our analysis.

Our study will show that the textual allusions to Psalm 23 found in Lamentations 1 are mainly of a polemic nature, which in

---

8. Steiner, "L'écriture de l'inconsolable," 11–12.

9. Sommer, *A Prophet Reads Scripture*. Cited in Tiemeyer, "Two Prophets, Two Laments," 191.

10. Bakhtin, *Speech Genres*, 91. Cited in Mandolfo, "Dialogic Form Criticism," 73.

the aggregate depict God as the anti-shepherd. This presentation has to contend, however, with the fact that nowhere in Lamentations 1 is God referred to as shepherd nor is Israel called sheep. It is by the depth of the language in the psalm permeating the lament that an appreciation of its polemical use is gained. Lamentations 1 alludes to and reverses the pastoral terminology present in Psalm 23.[11]

Our exploration takes on added significance when viewed from the common depiction of Israel's leaders as shepherds. A frequent explanation the prophets used to make sense of Israel's defeat and exile is that its shepherds were corrupt and faithless in carrying out their duties of watching over the nation. Ezekiel 34, Jeremiah 23, and Zechariah 10–11 are examples of this prophetic interpretation of history.[12]

Lamentations 1 does not follow this thinking. Instead, the poem frankly recognizes both the necessity of Israel's alliances with foreign nations to defend itself from the encroachments of the overwhelming might of the Babylonian empire, however futile those alliances were. It acknowledges and takes responsibility for the compromises required by these alliances which called down prophetic judgment. It mourns the inability of Israel's leadership and its warriors to defend the nation against overwhelming might, leaving it totally vulnerable to the excesses of suffering at the hands of the Babylonian army. On the contrary, Lamentations 1 criticizes God for being the anti-shepherd, leaving Zion and her children to unspeakable horrors.[13]

Before proceeding, some notice of the relative dating of Psalm 23 to Lamentations 1 is in order. On the time of composition of Lamentations there is general agreement that it happened shortly after the destruction of Jerusalem, the sacking of the temple, and the deportation of the ruling class in the first quarter of the sixth century BCE. Dating the writing of Psalm 23 is notoriously difficult, and scholarly proposals diverge widely. In his investigation of the psalm's influence on Lamentations 3, van Hecke notes that "in

11. See a similar approach in Van Hecke, "Lamentations 3:1–6," 267.
12. Childs, "Retrospective Reading."
13. See Parry, "Lamentations and the Poetic Politics of Prayer," 80.

his standard commentary Kraus argues that the Psalm must have originated in preexilic Jerusalem, even though it was used time and time again as a formulary prayer in later periods" and he can find no "conclusive reasons to discard at once the chronological possibility of the influence of Ps 23 on Lam 3."[14] With that cautious possibility in hand, we will explore this relationship.

Like a wail that never stops, the absence of a comforter dots the landscape of the lament. The city "has no one to comfort her" (v. 2); "none to comfort her" (v. 9); she weeps "for a comforter is far from me" (v. 16); "Zion stretches out her hands, but there is no one to comfort her" (v. 17); her enemies "heard how I was groaning with no one to comfort me" (v. 21). "Comforter" is the participle of the verb נחם in its pi'el conjugation. It appears in Psalm 23:4 as "they comfort me," referring to the shepherd's rod and staff. The glaring lack of protection from God, the shepherd who comforts, for Jerusalem/Zion is central to her groaning. In v. 17 the absence of God as comforter is punctuated by the following line "the LORD has commanded against Jacob."

In tandem with the shared motif of God as comforter/anti-comforter is that of God as restorer/non-restorer of soul/strength/ life. As has been noted, Safren pointed to the similarity between נפשי ישובב "he restores my soul" in Psalm 23:3a to נפש להשיב "to revive their strength" in Lamentations 1:11 and נפשם את וישיבו "to keep alive"[15] in Lamentations 1:19. In Lamentations 1:16 the absent comforter of Zion is described as "my reviver" משיב נפשי. That the absence of the comforter and the absence of one to keep alive are meant to interpret each other may be deduced from the unique arrangement of Lamentations 1:9–12, discussed earlier, into two parallel sets of v. 9ab/vv. 9c–10 and v. 11ab/vv. 11c–12. Verse 9b underscores the lack of a comforter and v. 11b that of the futile efforts to revive strength. Each of these lines are followed by extended imperatives for the Lord to take notice. Again, the

---

14. Van Hecke, "Lamentations 3:1–6," 276.

15. Translating the Hiphi'il imperfect of שוב "to bring back" as in infinitive based on the fact that ו + the imperfect can indicate the intention of an action, Renkema, *Lamentations*, 185.

co-functionality of being a comforter and reviver of soul/courage are displayed in parallel to each other in v. 16, a verse that explodes in groaning. So, two of the main functions ascribed to the shepherd in Psalm 23, that of restoring of life and the protection of a comforter, are specifically called out as lacking in God's response to Zion's plight, adding to the burden of pain that can only finally be discharged in groaning.

A third link between the two texts is found in the shared use of the verb רדף "to pursue/persecute." Psalm 23:4 uses the striking metaphor of the forces of "goodness and mercy" pushing forward to hurry the speaker "all the days of my life" into the house of the LORD to dwell forever. The participial form is chosen by the poet of Lamentations 1:3 to describe Judah's pursuers overtaking her in the midst of her distress, and in v. 6 Zion's princes scattered "before the pursuer." Here the poet takes the received psalm text and inverts its intent to describe chaos and disintegration.[16]

Another illustration of a common word being used for contrasting effects is נוח "to rest." This verb is the root for נאות "pasture" and מנחות "still" in Psalm 23:2. The green pasture and still waters support the statement of v. 3, "he restores my soul." In Lamentations 1:3 Judah "finds no resting place" מנוח. Thus two borrowings from Psalm 23 are paired in Lamentations 1:3—no pasture מנוח and being overrun by pursuers רדפיה—to describe the distress of Judah. This thought is repeated with similar wording in v. 6bc, "Her princes have become like stags that find no pasture (מרעה); they fled without strength (כח) before the pursuer (רודף)." This motif of dire food insecurity is repeated twice again in Lamentations 1:11, the poem's central verse, and in the coda, v. 19.

To summarize, in ten verses of Lamentations 1 the poet has used four words that call to mind key words from the beloved psalm of the shepherd. These four words are redolent with meaning that supports the picture of God as specially caring for Israel. They attract to themselves additional layers of positive meaning

16. Van Hecke, "Lamentations 3:1–6," 268, points to a similar allusion to the comfort of the shepherd's rod in Psalm 23:4b now appearing in Lamentations 3:1–2 as the rod that drives into affliction.

from the context in which they appear in the psalm. In every case the poet of the lament has inverted their positive intention to make plain the absence of God's response to the pain of Zion.

Widening our investigation to consider broader themes, take note that the climax of the psalm "and I will dwell in the house of the LORD all my days" disintegrates in Lamentations 1:10 with the picture of the nations invading Zion's sanctuary "the house of the LORD."[17] We have already indicated the possible analogy of sexual violation in the occupation and desecration of the temple. The psalm's happy prospect of unending residence in the house of the LORD "all my days" is twisted in Lamentations 1:13 to Zion's being stunned "all day long" by God the warrior.

Another noteworthy thematic overlap occurs in the multiple ways the lament trounces on the psalm's confident "you are with me." In the lament the LORD "has made her [Zion] suffer" (v. 5); "handed me over" (v. 14); "has rejected all my warriors . . . trodden . . . the virgin daughter" (v. 15); "has commanded against Jacob" (v. 17); "is in the right" (v. 18). Verse 13 is devoted entirely to hostile acts of the LORD against Zion: sending fire, spreading a net, turning back, leaving stunned and faint all day long.[18]

Finally, the lament draws out other contrasts: Look at the contrast between a frantic, futile search for food (vv. 6, 7, 11, 19) and the shepherd's leading sheep into pasture and water. The house of death (v. 20) replaces the house of the LORD.[19] And, while in the psalm the table spread before my enemies is designed to show God's elevating the speaker to dominance, in the lament the roles are reversed where in the absence of a helper (עוזר)[20] "the foe looked on mocking over her downfall."

In sum, whereas any single citation of probable association of Psalm 23 with Lamentations 1 would be dubious grounds in

17. Van Hecke, "Lamentations 3:1–6," 271, discusses a similar association with the house of the LORD and the house of darkness.

18. Thomas, "Lamentations and the Trustworthiness of God."

19. Van Hecke, "Lamentations 3:1–6," 270, points out Psalm 49:14, "death shall be their shepherd."

20. God is frequently described by forms of the verb עזר.

arguing for interdependence, the preponderance of shared words, phrases, and themes speaks strongly for the rendering of God as the anti-shepherd and the lament as the anti-psalm. This literary portrayal of God was linked with groaning as hermeneutical keys for the collection.

Van Hecke asks: Were the authors of Lamentations likely to have referred to one of the Psalms in constructing their text? He points to "general agreement among scholars that these biblical authors were very well versed in the language of the psalms, using terminology and words taken from the psalms in their own compositions." This suggests to him that authors were to be sought among the temple singers for whom the singing of the psalms used to be a daily task, but who were now left in Jerusalem after the destruction of the temple.[21] He advances the conclusion that "the authors of Lamentations thus appear to have had a profound knowledge of the theology and the language of the psalms, while it was a normal practice for these authors to dialogue with or to oppose the religious thinking of the psalms."[22]

This suggestion resonates with the program of dialogic linguistics, already referenced, developed by Mikhail Bakhtin: "Every utterance must be regarded primarily as a response to preceding utterances of the given sphere. . . . Each utterance refutes, affirms, supplements, and relies on the others, presupposes them to be known, and somehow takes them into account. . . . It is impossible to determine its position without correlating it with other positions."[23] If the author of Lamentations 1 were a groaning priest, famished, stunned, and faint, he has surely found his voice in turning inside out the trust in God that is richly celebrated in Psalm 23 to protest against God's cruelly disproportionate punishment for Zion's sin.

---

21. It may be significant in this regard that in the psalm verbs used in the basic conjugations of the qal and pi'el appear in the lament in derived forms such as participles and Hiphi'il infinitive.

22. Van Hecke, "Lamentations 3:1–6," 276. Hillers, *Lamentations*, 111–12, lists sixty psalms alluded to in the book of Lamentations.

23. Bakhtin, *Speech Genres*.

As a case in point, the nations with whom Zion allies herself are viewed as her lovers, which in the prophetic tradition makes them illustrations of her infidelity to the Lord. Alliances that seemed prudent and inescapable on the political level were judged by the prophets to be "adulterous," justifying the punishment she received. Her lovers betrayed and deceived her (Lam 1:2, 7, 17, 19) adding to her burden of degradation. However, these verses include a "talk back" using the key word from Psalm 23 "comfort" or its synonym, "helper." The charge is that no one has come to Zion's rescue after the nations with whom she was in alliance abandoned her. The prophetic critique of Zion's alliances serves as the background to push to the forefront the anti-shepherd's non-response. Thus Lamentations 1 is an example of Bakhtin's understanding of double-voiced discourse, when the voice of the psalm is recontextualized in the speech of the groaning priest.

Carleen Mandolfo asks: what does it mean, theologically, when the voice traditionally representing the divine position, the voice of authority, speaks against its own interests and from the perspective of suffering humans?[24] Certainly, the reversal of the shepherd metaphor must have had "a strongly undermining and iconoclastic effect on contemporary theological reasoning."[25] Results from the field of trauma studies bear up this thought. "Catastrophic losses, extreme damage to familiar relationships, networks, structures, and systems are trauma-causing realities that often leave communities with feelings of betrayal and abandonment, especially when the perpetrating structures, groups, or individuals were expected to be defenders or protectors."[26]

24. Mandolfo, "Dialogic Form Criticism," 85.

25. Van Hecke, "Lamentations 3:1–6," 279. Scott, *Domination and the Arts of Resistance*, 67: "Those renegade members of the dominant elite who ignore the standard script . . . present a danger [to the status quo] far greater than their miniscule numbers might imply." Cited in Mandolfo, "Dialogic Form Criticism," 91.

26. Yansen, *Daughter Zion's Trauma*, 30. See also her discussion on p. 34. The suggestion might be offered that under the stress of trauma these feelings were unfortunately mistaken, that God was truly not the anti-shepherd the laments described. See the earlier discussion in the introduction about cognitive

The picture of the anti-shepherd God, in tandem with groaning, guides the reader on how to read the entire collection. The anti-shepherd shows up again dramatically in Lamentations 3:1–6, in the pivotal position at the center of the book, and Lamentations 4 and 5 hammer home the degradation of Yahweh's "flock." The reader finishes the fifth poem with the signature word of the first poem borrowed from the psalm ringing in the ear, "Restore us to yourself, O LORD, that we may be restored, renew our days as of old." However, the terrifying possibility created by the reverse exegesis of Psalm 23 supports the book's final words that haunt forever: "For if truly you have rejected us, raging bitterly against us—then . . . ."

In sum, it has often been noticed that Psalms 22 and 23 are intentionally paired, with Psalm 23 being the confident affirmation of God's presence to the lament of Psalm 22 that voices God's abandonment.[27] Lamentations 1 destroys the linkage by using Psalm 23 to construct a lament to God as the anti-shepherd. This symbol anchors a new "master narrative" by which Israel is to understand itself as it strives to survive in its new exilic state. As exiles of the anti-shepherd God, its ritual practices will be in the form of the lament, which will convey the full range of anger, doubt, protest, cajoling, and accusation. While some might observe that this new symbol is evidence of typical survival processes, such as displacement, and thus what Israel is saying may not be reality, this may be too facile a conclusion. It will be demonstrated in the following sections how biblical interpreters come to grips with the evidence of God's declaration of abandonment of God's people.[28]

---

overload leading to distortion. Yet, counter-testimony in Isaiah 54:6–8 indicates that Israel did not think so. See further discussion below.

27. See, for example, Miller, *Interpreting the Psalms*, 112, 119.

28. This, of course, is not the only explanation given for Israel's collective trauma. We have pointed to at least two others; exile as punishment for sin (self-blaming) and the betrayal of Israel's "lovers," the nations in which it was in alliance (transference).

The Afterlife of Lamentations 1 in Isaiah 40

The open-endedness of the close of Lamentations is generally recognized even though unanimity is lacking in the translations of this "if" fragment without a "then" to complete it. The book literally cries out for a response. It is "a lament straining towards life."[29] Linafelt comments: "But, to my mind, it is of the utmost importance that this judgment [the unfulfilled 'then'] is left unstated, and therefore the vision of the future, while hardly bright at this point in the poetry, is nevertheless left open."[30] It is a hope in search of confirmation, and the righteousness of God is at stake. Parry points out that "there is a strong sense in which . . . texts do not see their meaning as closed but open to being perceived afresh as the story continues to unfold." He notices "that many biblical books lack a sense of closure but look forward to the ongoing story which will unfold." Consistent with what we are about to explore is "the inner-biblical reuse of earlier traditions and texts in fresh ways to fit the changing context of the story. . . . Old stories are invited to be read against the expanding horizon of the grand story of God's relationship with his people as it moves ever onward."[31]

A study of communities in Israel that read and reworked their textual tradition shows that they carefully honored the form of the text they read while shaping a fresh reading of their tradition to respond to the context in which they read.[32] Focusing on the community that inherited Lamentations at the time of the lifting of the exile under the Persian empire, many commentators have pointed to the use Isaiah 40–55 (the so-called Second Isaiah) makes of Lamentations.[33]

Parry reminds that

29. Parry, "Wresting with Lamentations," 127.

30. Linafelt, "Surviving Lamentations (One More Time)," 58.

31. Parry "Prolegomena," 400.

32. Parry, "Wrestling with Lamentations," 137.

33. In a footnote, Tiemeyer, "Two Prophets, Two Laments," 187, sums up: "The textual and conceptual links between Is 40–55 and Lamentations have long been known." See, as examples, Linafelt, *Surviving Lamentations*; and Willey, *Remember the Former Things*.

the prophet of Isaiah 40–55 is usually thought to have prophesied towards the end of Israel's exilic period. He clearly anticipates the end of the period of suffering so acutely given voice in Lamentations. As part of his message he seems to have quite consciously taken up the text of Lamentations. Second Isaiah clearly sees himself as announcing Yahweh's response to the pain of Jerusalem expressed in Lamentations. Texts from all five chapters of the lament are taken up and reused in the prophecy and the overall effect is one of *radical reversal* for Jerusalem.[34]

Tiemeyer proposes a liturgical setting for the reading of Lamentations where the writers of Isaiah 40–55 could have had access to it. She advances a probable liturgical setting similar to that described in Zechariah 7:3, 5. She bases this proposal on the similarities between Lamentations and Isaiah with lament psalms. "It is reasonable," she concludes, "to assume that Lamentations was well-known to the Deutero-Isaiah group."[35] It is time now to examine Second Isaiah's response to Lamentations 1.

Isaiah 40 begins with the call, "Comfort, comfort my people, says your God. Speak tenderly to Jerusalem and cry to her that her warfare is ended, that her iniquity is pardoned, that she has received from the LORD's hand, double for all her sins." This verse announces the hermeneutical perspective from which chapters 40–55 are to be read: an urgent, passionate reaching out of God to a dispirited, cynical people. This is a reading community that has been deeply influenced by the liturgical shaping of Lamentations 1 to groan in despair over the absence of a comforter. This is mentioned six times in Lamentations 1. As we have demonstrated, the absent comforter is the reverse of the shepherd's role in Psalm 23. Isaiah 40–55 begins to fill the void left by the "unless . . ." at the end of Lamentations, and Isaiah 40:1 now links up with Lamentations 1 so that the comforter bursts on the scene again to respond to Lady Jerusalem's pleas to see her sorrow and do something

---

34. Parry, "Prolegomena," 401.

35. Tiemeyer, "Two Prophets, Two Laments," 190. See also Parry, "Lamentations and the Poetic Politics of Prayer."

about it. Isaiah 54:6–8 is foundational for understanding this announcement:[36]

> For the LORD has called you
>> like a wife forsaken and grieved in spirit,
> like the wife of a man's youth when she is cast off,
>> says your God.
> For a brief moment I abandoned you,
>> but with great compassion I will gather you.
> In overflowing wrath for a moment
>> I hid my face from you,
> but with everlasting love I will have compassion on you,
>> says the LORD, your Redeemer.

It is hard to overestimate the importance of this self-avowal from God for comprehending the shift in the picture of God as the anti-shepherd. As Lamentations 5:21–22 indicates, Israel clearly understands that in the destruction of 587 BCE, God has made a move toward terminating the covenantal relationship by becoming the anti-shepherd. Israel also understands that God's self-regard—that is, God's defense of God's glory, holiness, and jealousy perhaps—requires God to become the anti-shepherd.

However, as seen in God's self-avowal above, God does not irreversibly stay the anti-shepherd. Indeed, what seemed to be complete abandonment was in fact "for a moment." Israel survived the anti-shepherd God, because it protested the excesses, the injustices, of the anti-shepherd. Their outcry for a witness had the effect of deepening God's covenantal engagement and intensifying God's positive passion for Israel right at the moment when God was poised to walk away. Thus the depth of passion turned from acts of jealousy to a commitment "to suffer with and to suffer for, to be in solidarity with Israel in its suffering, and by such solidarity to sustain a relationship that rightfully could be terminated."[37]

36. See Brueggemann, "A Shattered Transcendence," and Brueggemann, *Theology*, 298–99.

37. Brueggemann, *Theology*, 299. This text underscores the unique role Israel plays in the ongoing revealing of God's nature and cautions against attempts to understand any other instance of personal, national, or ethnic suffering in terms of God's abandonment.

God became a witness, a helper, because God found in God's own internal life a depth of devotion to the well-being of Israel that was not, until that moment of crisis, available to God.

It is significant that later in Isaiah 40:11 this comforter is specifically called "a shepherd" and Israel "his flock." Thus Isaiah 40:1–2 begins the engagement to deconstruct the image of God in Lamentations 1 and to replace it with a fresh reading of the shepherd. The shepherd is described as "feeding" his flock. This has the effect of moving the reading community beyond being fixated on hunger, famine, death, fatigue. It reinvigorates the restorative function of the shepherd, speaking directly to the multiple instances of the dire lack of restoration in Lamentations 1.

The sufferings of exiled Mother Zion were compounded by the loss of her children. They were taken into captivity (Lam 1:5), they wandered (Lam 1:7), they died in the famine (Lam 1:19), they were slaughtered at home (Lam 1:20). This imagery is the reverse of the faithfulness of the shepherd-Lord of Psalm 23. As the postexilic community grasped the opportunity to rehabilitate the shepherd image, so the writer(s) of Isaiah 40–55 wanted to set right Israel's expectations of how their shepherd would relate to his flock. Isaiah 40:11 upends Lamentations' reversal of Psalm 23 by describing how the shepherd gathers the lambs and carries them in his bosom and gently leads the mother sheep.[38] Zion will be amazed at all the children she has and will wonder where they came from (Isa 49:21). Isaiah 40:10 makes plain that the restoration of Zion to her children comes about because of the unassailable protection of the Lord's might and arm. It is not unreasonable to interpret this as a reference to the shepherd's rod and staff of the psalm.

38. This foregrounding of the shepherd who leads in a nurturing way in Isaiah 40 balances Second Isaiah's use of the metaphor of the nursing mother: "Can a woman *forget* her nursing child that she would have no compassion on the son of her womb? Even these may forget, *yet I will not forget you*." Linafelt may be overstating when he writes, "The poet chooses here the one metaphor for Yahweh that can bring to answer the rhetoric of Lamentations. Yahweh as a mother who also laments and hopes for the return of her children" (*Surviving Lamentations*, 75; cited in Parry, "Prolegomena," 402).

We have demonstrated that the theme of the absence of a comforter/restorer of soul became an important ingredient in how to read Lamentations, and now we see how Isaiah 40 takes this on and transforms a despairing reading of Psalm 23 to bring a hermeneutic of hope. This transformation continues with the other piece of how to read Lamentations we highlighted, that of groaning (אנח). To recall, this behavior crops up five times and its physiological manifestation twice in Lamentations 1. It plays a major role in organizing not only Lamentations 1 but also by fixing the depth of passion to be attached to the four chapters that follow. We suggested that the strategic placement of "groaning" at four-verse intervals acted as a pressure valve to discharge a load of feeling beyond words that is created by the description of suffering.

The first of these four-verse sets presents an opportunity for the author(s) of Isaiah 40–55 to address this fundamental pillar of reading Lamentations. In Lamentations 1:3–4, "pursuers" (רדף Qal participle) "overtook" (נשג in Hiph) Zion and imposed "suffering" and "groaning" (אנח in Niph) on her.[39] This is in contrast to the striking metaphor of Psalm 23:4 where the forces of "goodness and mercy" push forward (רדף) to hurry the speaker "all the days of my life" into the house of the LORD to dwell forever. But now Second Isaiah makes plain that gladness "overtakes" (נשג in Hiph) her and "suffering" and "groaning" (אנח in Niph) flee away (Isa 51:11).

It is plausible that the poet of Isaiah 40 was aware of the need to engage the awful spectacle of the degradation and humiliation of Lady Jerusalem by her enemies evidenced by their mockingly leering at her in Lamentations 1:7. We advanced the view that Psalm 23:5, where the LORD as shepherd arranged for a similar happening to the psalm-speaker's enemies, was being upended as another instance of God as the anti-shepherd. This outrage placed upon Lady Jerusalem could well be part of her cry at Lamentations 1:21–22 for God to enact retribution upon her enemies.

Isaiah 40:10–11 link the work of the nurturing shepherd with the coming of the LORD, who rules with a mighty arm to deliver

39. Parry cites this in "Prolegomena," 401.

recompense. This amounts to a reaffirmation of the psalm's imagery. While later chapters in Second Isaiah will describe how Babylon receives at the LORD's hand all that was meted out to Israel, the beginning of the reversal of Israel's humiliation, pictured in Lamentations, is anticipated in these opening verses. The deconstruction of the anti-shepherd continues apace.

This concern to re-present God as Israel's nurturing and protecting shepherd, however, does not blind the author(s) of Isaiah 40–55 to the stubborn reality of Israel's sin which was confessed so openly in Lamentations 1:8: "Jerusalem sinned grievously, so she has become a mockery." This reality is faced and dealt with in the most unexpected way in the song of the suffering servant (Isa 52:13—53:12).[40]

After describing the utter humiliation of the LORD's servant in Isaiah 53:3, the poet makes the startling turn to depict the servant in absolute solidarity with his audience. The poet is frankly astonished by this connection. Whereas common assumption held that the humiliation of the servant was punishment for his transgressions (an assumption shared by Lamentations 1), in fact the servant suffered because he bore the transgressions of the poet and his audience (Isa 53:4–5). This insight is epitomized by a borrowing from the imagery of the shepherd and sheep. "All we like sheep have gone astray, we have all turned to our own way, and the LORD has laid on him the iniquity of us all" (Isa 53:6). The servant becomes the embodiment of the fate of the sheep.

This suffering servant is called by God to receive all the suffering of the eponymous man of Lamentations 3 and, derivatively, the suffering of Lady Jerusalem/Zion in the surrounding chapters. In contradistinction to Lamentations 3:33, "for [the LORD] does not willingly afflict or grieve anyone" (an assertion made more prominent by its location at the midpoint of this chapter), Isaiah 53:10 counters, "Yet it was the will of the LORD to crush him with pain." "Upon him was the punishment that made us whole, and by his bruises we are healed" (Isa 53:5). This shocking theological

---

40. Parry summarizes the relationship of the Everyman of Lamentations 3 and the servant of the LORD in Isaiah in "Prolegomena," 402–3.

reflection within the servant song roots God within the depths of human sin as God assigns God's especially nominated man to bear the sufferings of an entire people in order that in its place restoration can come to Zion.

In sum, following Lamentations into its engagement with a hermeneutic of hope in Second Isaiah makes plain that both sin and suffering, both guilt and grievance expressed in the groaning are confronted, honored, and transformed in astonishing ways. Great creativity is exerted in extracting, honoring, and reversing the suffering by reviving the beloved imagery of Psalm 23 in Isaiah 40 to lay against Zion's degrading pain and her trenchant criticism of God in Lamentations 1. It is particularly noteworthy, in light of Zion's bewailing the loss of her children in Lamentations and God's coming forth as the nurturing shepherd in Isaiah 40, that the servant "shall see his offspring, and shall prolong his days; through him the will of the LORD shall prosper" (Isa 53:10).[41]

The Afterlife of Lamentations 1 in the New Testament

When the Christian church declares that its Bible is an entity comprising the Scriptures of Israel and the writings of the early church, which it calls the Old Testament and the New Testament, it is making a self-conscious confessional statement. It is declaring that it listens for God's Word by taking as its canon of authority both, equally, Old and New Testaments. The church reads the witness of the Old Testament in light of God's new revelation in Jesus Christ.

41. This, of course, is not the only place in the Old Testament where the testimony to God's engagement with despair occurs. I have argued in *Living in the Language of God* that the theology of the Book of the Twelve is framed by the questions "Truly the day of the LORD is great; terrible indeed—who can endure it?" (Joel 2:11) and "Where is the God of justice?" (Mal 2:17). These questions are emblematic of the continuing struggle of postexilic and diasporic Israel to confront both the ongoing evidence of the incapability of Israel to meet its covenantal responsibilities and the impotence of God to live up to God's covenantal obligations as expressed in Exodus 34. The resolution of this crisis comes as God takes responsibility to bring speech to Israel's lips (Hos 14) that fulfils both Israel's expectation to praise God and proves God's capability to bless God's people.

Conversely, the revelation of Jesus is only fully grasped in the context of the Scriptures of Israel. Under this fresh reading, then, certain resonances are established between God's presence in the life of Israel and the person and ministry of Jesus Christ. This type of reading is broadly canonical. When reading the Old Testament, canonical interpreters pay attention to honor both the integrity of the form of the text as well as the new canonical context in which the text is read. When reading the New Testament, canonical interpreters pay attention to how God's act in Jesus Christ engages the open-endedness of Israel's Scripture. To this point, the full force of the pain and accusations of Lamentations will be carefully respected in the way it is received by and responded to in light of God's act in Jesus Christ.[42]

To recall, the witness who responds to the cry from Lady Zion—"Look! See!" (Lam 1:9, 11–12)—receives a positive answer in the form of the nurturing shepherd in Isaiah 40:11, and the groaning of exilic Israel, mentioned seven times in Lamentations 1, is registered and responded to with the prophet's words of comfort and joy in Isaiah 51:11. Key to this happening is God's strange nomination of God's servant to embody and sum up the transgressions of the sheep who have gone astray, and the servant's death to open the way for Zion's children to come home. Thus the suffering servant can be the spokesperson for the laments of Zion's scattered children in Lamentations, paying attention to their pain and sorrow, even as he becomes the agency, at the cost of his life, of relieving that pain and sorrow.

Extensive scholarly work shows how Isaiah 40–55 has exerted more influence on the developing Christology of the New Testament than perhaps any other part of the Old Testament. Because of its linkage with Lamentations, Second Isaiah becomes a canonical bridge between Christian theology and Lamentations.[43]

---

42. Parry has written extensively on the canonical relationship of Lamentations within the Christian canon. See "Wrestling with Lamentations," 137, and "Prolegomena," 400.

43. Parry, "Prolegomena," 401.

Our investigation is following how the figure of the anti-shepherd and the behavior of groaning of Lamentations 1, as they are mediated through engagement with Second Isaiah, contribute significantly to the story of Jesus. We will attend to the behavior of groaning first.

This book makes the argument that the groaning of Lamentations 1 is contextualized and transformed in Second Isaiah as the servant obediently embraces the nature and fate of the wayward sheep. This identification plunges the servant into the cries of the wandering sheep of Lamentations. As such, he speaks out of and for the pain of Israel. Early Christians recognized soon how much the description of the servant helped them understand the ministry of Jesus, particularly his death and resurrection. When this linkage is recognized, one can see how each gospel reaches back at significant turning points to Isaiah 52–53 to underscore the solidarity Jesus takes on with those to whom he came. A short listing begins to show this significance.

- Matthew 8:17 summarizes a series of stories of Jesus' healing ministry with this quotation from Isaiah 53:4, "This was to fulfill what had been spoken through the prophet Isaiah, 'He took our infirmities and bore our diseases.'" Jesus becomes the chief witness to human pain and loss and the all-sufficient center to receive it.

- Mark 10:45 sets the stage for the final week of Jesus' life with the solemn pronouncement, "For the Son of Man came not to be served but to serve, and to give his life a ransom for many." While this announcement cannot be traced to a citation in the Old Testament, it attracts to it descriptions of the servant as the one who brings release from systemic encumbrances, servitudes, and constraints.

- Luke 23:34 recounts that as Jesus was being tortured to death by crucifixion, he prayed, "Father, forgive them; for they do not know what they are doing." Again, while not directly quoting from Isaiah, Jesus is shown enacting the servant's role as intercessor for transgressors. Furthermore, these words allude strongly to the human fog of unknowing that surrounds the strange working out of God's will.

- John 1:29 contains the first announcement by another human being, John the Baptist, of who Jesus is: "The next day he saw Jesus coming toward him and declared, 'Here is the Lamb of God who takes away the sin of the world!'" The reference to the lamb may be drawn from the sheep of Isaiah 53:7 whose non-resistance exemplifies the obedience of the servant and whose slaughter is a metaphor for the servant's pouring himself out to death as he "bore the sin of many" (Isa 53:12–13).

Ample evidence shows that early Christians, confronted with the shocking events of Jesus' life, death, and resurrection found helpful orientation in the suffering servant of Isaiah. Running through the evidence is the strong sense of solidarity between Jesus as God's servant and the people to whom he came. The burial of Jesus' corpse undertaken by Joseph of Arimathea (Matt 27:57) is correlated with Isaiah 53:9 "They made his grave with the wicked and his tomb with the rich." The resurrection brings to the forefront Isaiah 53:10–11 "When you make his life an offering for sin, he shall see his offspring, and shall prolong his days. . . . Out of his anguish he shall see light; he shall find satisfaction through his knowledge. . . . Therefore I will allot him a portion with the great, and he shall divide the spoil with the strong."

Thus, in light of the fact that the narrative of the suffering servant states twice that though "oppressed and . . . afflicted, yet he did not open his mouth; like a lamb that is led to the slaughter . . . is silent, so he did not open his mouth," it is highly significant that the narrative of Jesus' life deviates from the template and does not shirk from recalling him as not being silent, but being overcome by groaning.

The picture of him praying in the Garden of Gethsemane before his arrest, trial, and crucifixion contains the telltale signs of deep groaning. Jesus "began to be distressed and agitated." He said to trusted disciples, "I am deeply grieved, even to death; remain here, and keep awake." They, of course, did not (Mark 14:32–42).

Some manuscripts of Luke include that "in his anguish he prayed more earnestly, and his sweat became like great drops of blood falling down on the ground" (Luke 22:44). Dread of the torture and suffering anticipated is unmistakably what drives Jesus to the extremities of remaining in control of himself.

This memory of Jesus being assaulted by dread is reflected in Hebrews 5:7. The New Revised Standard Translation has: "In the days of his flesh, Jesus offered up prayers and supplications, with loud cries and tears, to the one who was able to save him from death, and he was heard because of his reverent submission." This reflection upon Jesus' ordeal in Gethsemane is part of the epistle's encouragement of its readers to engage God in bold prayer, as noted in Hebrews 3:6 (to hold firm to boldness of speech and boasting of hope) and 4:16 (to approach the throne of grace with bold frankness). In this context, Hebrews 5:7 portrays Jesus whose loud cries and weeping indicate that his prayers and supplications were sounds wrung from deep emotional places. His groaning was the badge of his reverence/obedience, which made his prayers comprehensible to God.[44] However, another rendering has it: "who, in the days of his flesh, offered prayers and supplications, with a loud cry and tears, to the One who was able to save him from death, and from his anxiety, [he] was heeded."[45] The import of this rendering would be to memorialize that God took heed to the abyss of anxiety as the root cause of Jesus' groaning.[46] The unmistakable impression is that while Jesus had to fight through his dread by groaning beyond words, God understood what his groans conveyed.

These remembrances of Jesus serve to illuminate the devastating plunge into the darkness of abandonment that enveloped Jesus in his final moments of torture by crucifixion. As the Gospel of Mark renders the ghastly scene, after Jesus cries, "My God,

44. See Attridge, "'Heard Because of His Reverence.'"

45. The Greek is *eisakoustheis àpò tῆs evlabelas*, and the notes in the commentary state that the usual translation of *àpò* is "from" rather than "because," and *evlabelas* is taken in its derived meaning of fear/anxiety.

46. Buchanan, *Hebrews*, 97–98.

my God, why have you forsaken me?" he gives up a loud cry and breathes his last (Mark 15:33–37) As has long been recognized, this cry repeats the opening verses of Psalm 22, one of nine lament psalms that are either quoted or alluded to in the passion narrative. Placing this cry in its broadest canonical context, Bauckham comments:

> In relating the passion and death of Jesus to the psalms of lament in general, Mark relates the passion and death of Jesus to the situation of all who wrote and used these psalms, those who cried out to God from the desperate situations those psalm describe. . . . [A] messianic reading of them would have to be *inclusively* messianic, i.e., referring to the way in which the experience of the Messiah gathers up into itself the experiences of all whose sufferings find expression in those psalms.[47]

Speaking canonically, Jesus prays the book of Lamentations not only alongside Zion but as well in solidarity with *all* whose structure of meaning have collapsed. In his final moments he knows the pain of living under an anti-shepherd.

By means of the wrenching cry of the crucified Jesus, the Son of God, joins in solidarity with all who find themselves transfixed in screaming rage. In his cry from the cross Jesus gathers up and speaks all human lament. The crush of the forsaken Zion we have been analyzing in Lamentations 1, now concentrated in the suffering servant, comes out in curdled sound from the Son who is abandoned by the Father.[48] On the cross, the groan of Jesus confirms the distance God fixes between the abandoning Father and his abandoned Son, and, through the Son, the way God spurns the world.[49] Parry confirms: "Jesus' experience of alienation from God was not simply an inner feeling of despair but the concrete reality

---

47. Bauckham "God's Self-Identification with the Godforsaken," 255.

48. See Parry, "Lamentations and the Poetic Politics of Prayer," 86: "The political death of Jesus on the cross places him in a canonical way as the symbolic gathering up of Zion's sufferings expressed in Lamentations."

49. See Bailey, *The Self-Shaming God Who Reconciles*, 70–73.

of suffering injustice, betrayal, torture, and defeat at the hands of those who worship false gods."[50]

Recalling that the final verse of Lamentations is that trembling spitting out of a horrifying possibility ("For if truly you have rejected us, raging bitterly against us—then . . ."; Lam 5:22), the groan from the cross supplies that which could not be spoken. The burial of Jesus "with the wicked and the rich" makes the "then" out to be the terror of God's betrayal of the obedient Son. Holy Saturday allows this terror to have its full power and sway. Holy Saturday is the passion narrative's embracing of the unthinkable "then" of Lamentations.[51]

The resurrection not only vindicates Jesus as truly the Son of God, but also God as really the loving Father of Jesus. Moreover, the astonishing and provocative message at the heart of resurrection is that God's utter identification in God's Son with the extremes of human suffering and God-abandonment is *willed* so that God's victory over all that reduces humans to groaning, shown in resurrecting the Son, can catch up with new life all persons who have been so pummeled.

God makes the very circumstances designed to grind humans down into submission become the context for experiencing the very thing they were designed to subvert. God goes to such radical lengths to take on the human and spiritual costs of being devalued so that God can redeem humanity from that fate. Thus, God proves that God is ultimately reliable, and that humans can take hope, even in darkest despair and screaming rage, that God's good intentions for humanity will prevail.

---

50. Parry, "The Trinity and Lament," 152. See Bauckham "God's Self-Identification," 257: "It is somewhat misleading to say—of the psalmist or of Jesus echoing his words—that he feels forsaken by God as though this were an understandable mistake, . . . not merely in psychological experience but in the form of the concrete situation that Jesus experiences." The extreme conditions under which he suffered did not lead him astray in his perception.

51. Parry, "Prolegomena," 414, affirms Alan E. Lewis's construal of Holy Saturday as God's allowing destruction and death a penultimate word. Holy Saturday allows the shock of the pain of abandonment to have its full force. See Lewis, *Between Cross and Resurrection*.

Lamentations are the words of those who are dangling on the edge of an unfulfilled conclusion ("For if . . . then . . ."). The religious and political life of postexilic Israel was suspended between the trauma of destruction and an unknown future. Christians read Lamentations similarly, in a state of unfulfillment. Christians wait for God to complete God's triumph over all that rebels against divine rule. As the world endured a Holy Saturday suspended between ghastly crucifixion and a gaping future, so our time is a version of Holy Saturday, suspended between the Easter triumph and the eschaton. This suspension is filled with both hope and fear, both goodness and trauma, both praise and lament. Groaning remains very much an inevitability for those who live in the moment of Holy Saturday. In solidarity with us, Jesus becomes the Christian's lamenter-in-chief, the one who speaks with us our groans in the voices of Lamentations.

It is important to remember that Jesus began his life in the cacophony of groaning.[52] The final episode in Matthew's nativity story tells of Herod's being tricked by the "wise men from the East" (Matt 2:1–18) and his murderous reprisal upon all boys of Bethlehem up to two years old. The narrative of this horror concludes with a quotation from Jeremiah:

> A voice was heard in Ramah,
>   wailing and loud lamentation,
> Rachel weeping for her children,
>   she refused to be consoled,
>   because they are no more.

We only have to recall that copious and unrelieved weeping are the physiological manifestations of groaning to see that this behavior stands at the beginning and end of the story of Jesus.

---

52. It is instructive to contrast the women's voices in the beginning of Jesus' life in Matthew with the voices of Mary and Elizabeth, both pregnant, in Luke. Upon Elizabeth's greeting of Mary, she sings, "My soul magnifies the Lord, and my spirit rejoices in God my Savior, for he has looked with favor on the lowliness of his servant. . . . For the Mighty One has done great things for me, and holy is his name" (Luke 1:46–49). Mary's praise of God as an active witness to her lowliness is a co-respondent by canonical logic to Lady Zion's unanswered crying for a witness.

I would suggest that canonical logic establishes a link between this unspeakable outrage and Lamentations.[53] Through this link the grinding privations that Lady Zion and her children endured at the hands of an implacable and out-of-control invading army flow into the sudden and profound suffering in Bethlehem created by the soldiers of a terrified and unsettled tyrant. The trauma was so great within the community, which helplessly watched children ripped from arms and killed, that it nullified the capacities of any consolation to Bethlehem. The uncontrolled groaning that issued forth is magnified when joined with Lady Zion's plea, "Look and see if there is any sorrow like my sorrow which was brought upon me." Moreover, the vast emptiness into which Bethlehem was plunged ("they are no more") reaches back to join with the way Lamentations peters out into a black-hole future ("if you are angry with us beyond measure, then . . ."). Both face a future that cannot be retrieved.

The inconsolable weeping in which the story of Jesus' life opens in Matthew has a mirror image in the Gospel of John at the end of Jesus' life with Mary's weeping at the entrance of an empty tomb (John 20:11–18). Not only is her Lord dead, but now the place to which she could go to be near his body is an empty cavern. Here John reduces the world of hurt to one woman's groaning at the collapse of her structure of meaning. She symbolizes all who are cruelly deprived of a future that cannot be retrieved.

The first move the resurrected Jesus makes is to act as a witness to her weeping with the question, "Woman, why are you weeping?" He follows up with saying her name, and this gesture enfolds into his resurrected-crucified body her sense of a future that cannot be retrieved while simultaneously reestablishing ongoing community with her. However, Jesus wards off Mary's attempts to hold on to him. He will lead her into learning how to live onward with him in the Spirit. This is the essence of the transformation of suffering within the crucified-resurrected Christ. Placing yourself within the body of the crucified-resurrected Jesus you may find the promise of transformation so that the trauma that

---

53. See, generally, Wainwright, "Rachel Weeping for Her Children."

never goes away becomes the site from which one can creatively move forward in one's life.

As the story of Jesus affirms God's joining with the hurt of the world to provide healing, so that same story opens up a possibility of transforming the figure of God as anti-shepherd. We have suggested that the Lady Zion's cries over her displaced and dead children join with the parents of Bethlehem. Canonical logic would urge that the comfort of Isaiah 40:11 to Zion is available to those in Bethlehem who must live with a future that cannot be reversed. "He [the LORD] will feed his flock like a shepherd, he will gather the lambs in his arms, and carry them in his bosom, and gently lead the mother sheep." What would this comfort in the midst of irreversible loss look like? The rehabilitation of God from being the anti-shepherd that happens in the story of Jesus as the Good Shepherd (John 10:1–18) may give us a clue toward an answer.

Isaiah 40:11, along with material from Psalm 23, Ezekiel 34, and Hosea 11, provide the imagery for the figure of Jesus as the good shepherd. It is clear to me that the symbol acts as a counterfoil to the anti-shepherd of Lamentations. The comfort that was so lacking in Lamentations 1 is brought out in the description of the good shepherd. The sheep hear and recognize his voice; he calls his sheep by name; they follow willingly; he leads them out to good pasture. Yet, how does this reappearance of God as shepherd change the situation for those who groan for a future that cannot be retrieved?

The acts of the anti-shepherd in Lamentations 1 are reversed by the good shepherd. However, what is new to this collection of descriptors that rehabilitate God as shepherd is the assertion from the good shepherd that he lays down his life for the sheep to protect them. This, plainly, was not something expected by the community that read Lamentations. This, of course, does resonate with the suffering servant of Isaiah 53 who becomes like the straying sheep and dies for their transgression. The metaphors become mixed as the good shepherd gives away his life protecting his sheep from predators, while the suffering servant obediently dies by the hand of God to make it possible for exiles to return to Zion.

Yet the two texts come together in the astonishing transformation of the aftermath. Even in death, the shepherd retains power to take up his life again, and the suffering servant shall prosper beyond the tomb. This is a striking occurrence of life that defies the power of death to close any access to a future. The shepherd and the servant coalesce in Jesus as the bringer of a new future into a situation of no-future. What finally makes the shepherd good, however, is the shepherd's ongoing work to bring in sheep not of his original flock. The shepherd is good because he creates a new flock out of the wreckage of the scattered sheep.

He welcomes us into his flock that flourishes strangely even within the wreckage of what is no longer viable, and for that hope we hang on for dear life. Jesus draws our loss into God's own self and absorbs its full shock into his crucified body. Then, God raises the wreckage of that groaning, betrayed, beaten, stripped-naked, and publicly humiliated body to demonstrate that Jesus is the source of new life out of the wreckage of what is no longer viable. Our worship entwines our lamenting between songs of praise, and we become people of creativity, stamina, grit, and verve.

Chapter 5

Black Theology as a Context for Transforming Groaning—I

James H. Cone and James H. Evans

Introduction

This foregoing interpretation of groaning in Lamentations and its canonical engagement was prompted by the raw reactions to the killing of George Floyd with which this book began. As I indicated in the introduction, I am not content to let this collection of profoundly disturbing responses be used anecdotally. Explicating the biblical notion of a witness raised by Lamentations makes me, the interpreter, a participant in the groaning of readers of this book, particularly Black religious readers. Whatever constructive thoughts I have must be forged in conversation with them.

In the next two chapters we will focus on resources in Black religion that engage deep, unspeakable hurt. I have selected to study and appreciate the work of James Cone, James Evers, Eddie Glaude Jr., and M. Shawn Copeland. They have been honest and caring guides to appreciating the wide range of Black religious thinking. I have come away with a much better understanding of the existential stakes in African Americans maintaining integrity against an oppressive system into which I was born and from which I have benefited. I gained a better appreciation of how these leaders shaped their theologies of survival against this system. In their capable hands, the figure of the witness took various shapes, but they all insisted that a witness must be engaged in order to press on toward freedom even as centuries-old scars were borne. In describing the way these thought leaders shape the role of the witness to groaning, Christology emerges as fundamental to how Jesus, as witness, contextualizes and transforms groaning.

Black theologians regularly argue that when Black people gather in congregations for worship what happens is critical to their resilience and stamina. The challenges are huge and unrelenting: how can a community maintain a positive sense of self-worth and a dogged and robust resistance to the aggressions of racial bias? People bring heavy burdens, grasping hopes, profound griefs, debilitating sins, and ecstatic joys to worship—all of which are bound up in the burden of degradation with its load of outrage against suffering brutality.

Often, the burden carried outstrips the capacity of words to express and can only be voiced in groaning, nevertheless they come expecting that their burdens will be woven into what happens there. What is reported often as happening is that as they give themselves to the flow of worship, their burdens become contextualized and transformed, resulting in their becoming different persons. Even with their burdens, they will be able to persevere in dignity and ultimately prevail in the justice they seek. Worship, therefore, is critically instrumental to their survival and flourishing.

Black worship has been studied carefully for the power it generates to support such transformation.[1] In this and the following chapter, we will explore four religious positions that give support and meaning to the contextualizing and transforming of groaning in the Black church experience. This chapter will consider a classical position represented by systematic theologians James H. Cone and James H. Evans. This will be followed in the next chapter by a survey of the work of Eddie Glaude Jr., whose study of

---

1. For a survey of major works studying Black worship, see Baldwin, "Deliverance to the Captives."

African American religion is informed by drawing on the work of James Baldwin and W. E. B. Du Bois. Finally, an analysis of the work of M. Shawn Copeland, a womanist theologian in the Roman Catholic tradition, concludes our survey.

These four thinkers are examples of the range of the theological and philosophical expression of Black religion. They represent distinctive understandings of how worship bridges the relationship between Christology and the human tragedy expressed in groaning. We will show how the functional Christology of Cone and Evans supports understanding worship as vectoring the burden of groaning away from the person to its overcoming in the resurrection thereby making the groaning one's striving for liberation possible despite their ambiguous situation. In Glaude's secularized "uncommon faith" groaning is contextualized within the womb of African ethnicity and history with its undying claims to liberty, justice, and right. By an act of sheer will the burden of groaning is transformed into renewed self-love and self-trust. Copeland draws deeply upon her Catholic spirituality of the continuing presence of the resurrected-crucified Jesus. Worship becomes the place where suffering is contextualized within this presence, which is sung, preached, and prayed. In that matrix, transformation of the one who groans happens such that hopeful defiance emerges. An exploration of these nuanced reflections on the relationship between Christology and groaning will sharpen the argument we are making.

James H. Cones and James H. Evans—Jesus as Liberator: A Functional Christology

Black theologian James H. Evans Jr. speaks for many pastors and students of Black worship: "The style, aesthetic, and creativity evident in the visible manifestations of Black religion are not merely the products of the artistic imagination of Black folk; they are also the attempts of the worshippers to envision new ideas, concepts, and cognitive paradigms for the interpretation of the world in which they live."[2]

Undergirding Black worship is a lived theology that grounds faith and dignity, providing the matrix that makes sense out of groaning in worship.[3] This theology is concentrated in the person and work of Jesus Christ. Thus, to understand how worship welcomes the groaning of deep trauma it is helpful to review some aspects of this example of classical Black Christology.

Generally speaking, Jesus is presented from the standpoint of what he *does* more than who he *is*. In a shorthand way, we might say that soteriology (the way Jesus acts as savior) sets the language of ontology (who Jesus is in his being).[4] We will use the term "functional Christology" to denominate this understanding of the Jesus who is known through what he does. Functional Christology presents Jesus from various perspectives: suffering servant, liberator, redeemer, conqueror, friend, and judge, to name the most prominent.

An understanding of the rise of functional Christology helps to understand the utility of this position. James Evans offers a perspective by citing an insight offered by Howard Thurman in 1949:

> I do not ignore the theological and metaphysical interpretation of the Christian doctrine of salvation. But the underprivileged everywhere have long since abandoned any hope that this type of salvation deals with the crucial issues by which their days are turned into despair without consolation. The basic fact is that Christianity as it was born in the mind of this Jewish thinker appears as a technique of survival for the oppressed. That it became, through the intervening years, a religion of the powerful and dominant, used sometimes as an instrument of

---

2. Evans, *We Have Been Believers*, 26.

3. Cone, *God of the Oppressed*, 1–38, and Evans, *We Have Been Believers*, 13–36.

4. Cone, *A Black Theology*, 119: "The soteriological value of Jesus' person must finally determine our christology." I am indebted to David J. Gouwens for drawing me to this citation. See also Evans, *We Have Been Believers*, 95.

oppression, must not tempt us into believing that it was thus in the mind and life of Jesus.[5]

The reader might be jarred by Thurman's calling Christianity a technique of survival for the oppressed, yet an observation by Stephen G. Ray Jr., in his introduction to Evans's systematic theology, places in historical perspective this identification of Christianity as a functional religion:

> A dominant narrative of the Christian faith in the African American community concerns how God came to the people as they were shut out from the main streams of the Christian faith in the United States, alienated from the texts of the tradition, and only introduced to Scripture as it was interpreted to legitimate their bondage. This communal narrative privileges the idea of the Spirit working immediately (unmediatedly, to be precise) and only derivatively by engaging with the texts of Scripture and tradition. . . . By starting his theology in the narrative of the believers, Evans grounds his entire project in this deep structure of African American Christian faith. This grounding then allows him to utilize the central category of Black Theology—liberation—as a hermeneutical device by which then to interpret the various loci of systematic theology.[6]

Making liberation the hermeneutical device to construe Christology sets up a trajectory to present the crucifixion and resurrection of Jesus as the death of a freedom fighter and his revolutionary victory over social and political powers that enslave human beings. This is picked up in 1968 by Albert Cleage in *The Black Messiah*. In opposition to the notion that Jesus was "white," Cleage judges this as "the crowning demonstration of their white supremacist conviction that all things good and valuable must be white."[7]

---

5. Evans, *We Have Been Believers*, 98, quoting Thurman, *Jesus and the Disinherited*, 28.

6. Evans, *We Have Been Believers*, xvi.

7. Cleage, *The Black Messiah*, 3. See Evans, *We Have Been Believers*, 99.

Evans explains this extreme position further:

> According to Cleage, African American people can never build the sense of dignity required to overcome oppression by worshipping a white Christ. In a radical rereading of the Bible Cleage argues that "the real Jesus," whose life is most accurately reported in the Synoptic Gospels, is not the false "spiritualized Jesus" reconstructed many years later by the Apostle Paul, who never knew Jesus and who modified Jesus' teachings to conform to the pagan philosophies of the "white gentiles."[8]

Evans presents functional Christology as an elliptical shape. The vindication of a crucified freedom fighter represents one of the two poles. Jesus is the liberator, the conqueror, the judge. He is the hero who now shares his hero status with believers. He is believable because he *once* was like them. His liberation, victory, and judgments are described as the freeing of Black people from a sociopolitical system that has supported and defended white supremacy.

The second pole of this elliptical Christology is rooted in Jesus' ministry to bring to light the indigenous spirituality and strength bequeathed to African Americans by God. This particular ethnic deposit becomes in Black Theology the kingdom of God. Bringing to light the kingdom of God within you is experienced as coming to proud awareness of what it means to be African by shaking off the crushing burden of otherness and difference. Thus, under the reign of Jesus, the hero, a Black society can emerge ruled by Black values of freedom, equality, and community. Within that society, confident that they share in Jesus' hero-status, his followers are impelled to join in the ongoing battle for freedom.

This elliptical Christology supports the rich worship tradition of the Black church to receive the burden of concerns carried by groaning. A very effective means for the meeting of Jesus and groaning in worship is through the singing of spirituals.[9] Singing

8. Evans, *We Have Been Believers*, 99–100, citing Cleage, *The Black Messiah*, 4.

9. I recognize that Black worship offers other effective means through

the spiritual, the singer integrates the burden of groaning with music and testimony of what Jesus does, which creates the possibility for transformation of the situation of the singer. Spirituals fuse belief and experience, surging up from the most passionate sympathy and understanding.[10] Baldwin expands this point:

> The story of Jesus' sufferings drew each slave who heard and believed it ever more deeply into the consciousness and particularity of his or her own experience. Bondsmen recognized the close parallels between Jesus' pain and grief and their own. Jesus, too, had been rejected and betrayed, had felt the sting of the lash, had shouldered a heavy load, had been hanged from a tree, and had been cursed and called everything but a child of god. In their picture of Calvary, the slaves imagined themselves as being there when Jesus died.[11]

This bond of empathy becomes the content of song:

> Were you there when they crucified my Lord? . . .
> Oh, sometimes is causes me to tremble, tremble, tremble. . . .

The dynamic of the spiritual's movement became the grounding for a functional Christology as people sang their convictions that as God was with Jesus when he experienced the agonies of the cross in solidarity with those for whom he had been fighting, so God is with me now in my struggles. I am strengthened by the presence of God with me, and Jesus resurrected gives my life meaning beyond history when such violence as slavery and lynching will be banished.[12]

---

which worshippers may express their traumas, such as intercessory prayer and personal testimony. Noteworthy is the enactment of being liberated, mediated through the act of preaching, where the speaker embodies the freedom hearers are seeking and the hearers participate in a call-and-response mode.

10. Baldwin, "Deliverance to the Captives," 32, cites Brown, "Negro Folk Expression," II, 212–13. See also the monumental work of Cone, *The Spirituals and the Blues*.

11. Baldwin, "Deliverance to the Captives," 32–33.

12. Cone, *The Cross and the Lynching Tree*, 21, 26.

Questions for Reflection

The history of the last four hundred years in North America and elsewhere has proven the effectiveness of a Black Christology infusing worship practices that bind together a community of resistance and advocacy against insurmountable odds. Even though I am someone whose white ethnicity and upbringing in the era of Jim Crow blocks my full appreciation of the burdens conveyed by the voices of Blacks, I am in awe of the power of Black worship to contextualize and transform this outrage beyond words.[13] It is in this spirit that I pose questions and make certain observations to offer for further discussion.

For example, does the exclusive emphasis on the Black experience for Christology leave undetermined the role, value, and destiny of non-Black persons? As we have seen from Thurman and Cleage, this quandary stems from a necessary rejection and anathematizing of the ideology of white supremacy and a suspicion of the motivations of any white overtures for mutual engagement.[14] Taking that into consideration, the question of the place of non-Black persons becomes urgent in the Christology of Cone.

> Jesus Christ is the subject of black Theology because he is the content of the hopes and dreams of black people. He ... has chosen them and thus became the foundation of their struggle for freedom. He was their Truth, enabling them to know that white definitions of Black humanity were lies. When their way became twisted and senseless, they told Jesus about it. He lifted their burdens and eased their pain, thereby bestowing upon them a vision of freedom that transcended historical limitations. ... There is no truth in Jesus Christ independent of the oppressed of the land—their history and culture. ... Indeed it can be said that to know Jesus is to know him as revealed in the struggle of the oppressed for freedom. Their struggle is Jesus' struggle and he is thus revealed

13. See Freedman, "Laying Claim to Sorrow beyond Words," B7.

14. Cone, *God of the Oppressed*, 217, states, "Our task is to be what we are in spite of white people, because we have seen the vision of freedom, and it is calling us to put the world in shape."

in the particularity of their cultural history—their hopes and dreams of freedom.[15]

While Cone argues rigorously for the Black experience being a full and necessary expression of the humanity of Jesus, he is careful not to state that it is a sufficient expression without remainder. As he put it: "The Black experience is a *source* of the truth but not the Truth itself. Jesus Christ is the Truth and thus stands in judgment over all statements about truth."[16] This gives him the footing to extend the grim realities of the Black people to include a metaphorical use that encompasses all of human wretchedness. Jesus discloses God's will "to be with humanity in our wretchedness."[17] This is a more expansive category than those victimized by race.

Yet, while I can appreciate the rigor of Cone's argument, it continues to raise questions about the limitations Black Christology places on the scope of the gospel proclamation that Christ dies for the ungodly (Rom 5:6). Cone states emphatically:

> The difference between Gerald Ford [the thirty-eighth President of the United States] and any black person is the distinction between the redeemed sinner and the unredeemed sinner. The struggle for freedom is God's struggle so the black person in the struggle for freedom is the redeemed sinner. A redeemed sinner recognizes that despite his participation in it, the world is unjust, and he must be committed to its liberation. An unredeemed sinner believes that the world is in good hands, and he enjoys his participation in it.[18]

Is Gerald Ford outside the scope of the radically universal gospel? Can we "deny to the oppressors their participation in the image of God, their freedom, their capacity for transformation"?[19] Does not such denial have the effect of making victimization of the racially oppressed the only mirror of Christ's suffering? Does not

15. Cone, *God of the Oppressed*, 32–34.

16. Cone, *God of the Oppressed*, 33.

17. Cone, *God of the Oppressed*, 35.

18. Cone, *God of the Oppressed*, 220.

19. Weddle, "The Liberator or Exorcist," 486.

such denial block consideration of the possibility that the ongoing mystery of Jesus Christ finally is that he continues to exist in some cosmic sense as the Lord over the field of eschatological possibilities for a new creation which includes the oppressors?

Likewise, limiting the scope of Christ's sufferings to solidarity with persons victimized by race has questionable implications for the shape of the liberation to be found in him. Cone cites, approvingly, a poem from Gerard Bissanthe:[20]

> From the despair of our cry,
> The heart's intensity,
> Out of death and dereliction
> In the land of our uprootedness,
> We shall one day give birth to our Christ,
> A Christ made flesh of our flesh,
> Our dark flesh of the Black people.

Cone rightly insists that "Truth cannot be separated from the people's struggle and the hopes and dreams that arise from that struggle."[21] That principle argues for a specific suffering becoming the template for the specifics of cosmic liberation. This move has the implication of extending the "Blackness" of that specific liberation beyond the limits of its ethnic grounds. Is the new creation that is to be found in Christ's resurrected-crucified body coterminous with or exhausted by what the liberation of Black people means?

The more serious question to put to a functional Christology, however, is the question of theodicy. This topic emerges out of the organization of functional Christology: (1) that just as God was with Jesus as he died a freedom fighter for the oppressed, so God is with Black persons who groan and struggle against the aggressions of white supremacy. (2) And, just as Jesus resurrected is the figure of a life fully freed and honored (the kingdom of God), so Jesus stands as the guarantee of a hope for a life fully freed and honored beyond death for all who accept him in humility and repentance.

---

20. Cone, *God of the Oppressed*, 16–17.

21. Cone, *God of the Oppressed*, 17.

As Cone acknowledges in his final book, this Christology generates a series of contradictions that continues to plague Black spirituality. "Blacks did not embrace the cross, however, without experiencing the profound contradictions that slavery, segregation and lynching posed for their faith."[22] He cites typical expressions of this struggle from Black history: "Why it was that thou didst look on with calm indifference of an unconcerned spectator, when thy holy law was violated, thy divine authority despised and a portion of thine own creatures reduced to a state of mere vassalage and misery!" And, "Sometimes it seems as though some wild beast had plunged his fangs into my heart, and was squeezing out its life-blood. Then I began to question the existence of God, and to say: 'If he does exist, is he just? If so, why does he suffer one race to oppress and enslave another, to rob them by unrighteous enactments of rights, which they hold most dear and sacred? . . . Is there no God?'"[23] He observes, "No historical situation was more challenging than the lynching era, when God the liberator seemed nowhere to be found." He comments, "Throughout the twentieth century, African Americans continued to struggle to reconcile their faith in God's justice and love with the persistence of Black suffering. Writer James Baldwin spoke for many, 'If [God's] love was so great, and if He loved all His children, why were we, the Blacks, cast down so far?' No one knows the answer to that question."[24]

Cone wrestled with this final challenge of theodicy throughout his life, which he lived passionately trying to find meaning in an absurd world of white supremacy: "What does the cross in the Christian scriptures and the Black experience of the blues have to say about these enduring atrocities? This is the question that both Black secular thought and prophetic faith seek to explain for the African American community, for America, and for the world."[25]

22. Cone, *The Cross and the Lynching Tree*, 26.

23. Cone, *The Cross and the Lynching Tree*, 27, cited Mays, *The Negro's God*, 43–44, 49.

24. Cone, *The Cross and the Lynching Tree*, 28, citing Baldwin, *The Fire Next Time*, 46.

25. Cone, *The Cross and the Lynching Tree*, 28.

It may be helpful in engaging this challenge of theodicy to recall how this functional Christology restricts the present work of Christ to be the figure of hope. His suffering has been accomplished, and he stands now as the glorious proof to the wretched of God's presence with them in their suffering. Christ's position then poses the question: If I am like Jesus, why am I still suffering? This question may fester in the sufferer, raising doubts about the sufficiency of their performance, such as not having shown sufficient humility and repentance before the holy God.

An opening from which one might address Cone's final challenge lies within his thoughtful meditation on the presence of the cross of Christ in the lynching tree of America extending into our current situation. At one point he references "the ongoing suffering and oppression of human beings" as "the crucified people of history," a descriptor coined by Ignacio Ellacuria, the Salvadoran martyr.[26] Later in his argument, speaking about Jesus' cross, he draws on a thought from the German New Testament scholar Ernst Käsemann: "The resurrection is . . . a chapter in the theology of the cross." Or the cross is "the signature of the one who is risen."[27] We want to bring these two thoughts in relationship with each other.

This has the effect of reversing the analogy. If the continued signature of the one who is risen is his crucified figure, then the resurrected-crucified Christ will continue to mirror those who are the crucified of history. It is not that humanity is like Jesus but that Jesus is like crucified humanity. This grounds the possibility we have been exploring all along, a new possibility that permits groaning to become enveloped into the great cry from the cross. As God in Christ continues to affirm with his broken body human brokenness, the broken ones are enveloped into the field of his eschatological possibilities, signified by a crucified body yet

26. Cone, *The Cross and the Lynching Tree*, xiv.

27. Cone, *The Cross and the Lynching Tree*, 26, citing Käsemann, "The Pauline Theology of the Cross," 172, and "The Saving Significance of the Death of Jesus in Paul," 56.

living. This possibility encourages openness and transparency in speaking of one's desperate circumstances.

Transforming Groaning in the Context of a Functional Christology

With these questions and observations in mind, we return to the fundamental question of how this functional Black Christology provides the grounds for the contextualizing and transforming of groaning in Black worship. If Black Christianity is a technique for survival, if the resurrection of a martyred freedom fighter imputes to the oppressed the freedom to struggle against suffering that destroys their humanity, how is groaning to be understood and what happens to groaning in worship? We would suggest two possible courses.

One possible construction is that groaning is a symptom and a marker of the oppression upon the bodies, minds, and spirits of its victims. Jesus Christ shows how God takes the burden of suffering off the shoulders of the oppressed. Cone explains:

> The pain of the oppressed is God's pain, for he takes their suffering as his own, thereby freeing them from its ultimate control of their lives. The oppressed do not have to worry about suffering because its power over their lives was defeated by God himself. God . . . took the humiliation and suffering of the oppressed into his own history. The divine event that happened on the cross liberated the oppressed to fight against suffering while not being determined by it.[28]

Groaning is contextualized by its power to determine being offloaded onto God's history as shown by Jesus Christ, seen throughout his ministry but especially on the cross. Groaning is taken up by God, thereby stripping its power to determine a negative outcome.

---

28. Cone, *God of the Oppressed*, 175.

Worship is, for many, the center for this contextualization and transformation. Again, Cone describes:

> Truth is . . . disclosed in the movement of the language and the passion created when a song is sung at the right pitch and tonal quality. Truth is found in shout, hum, and moan as these expressions move the people closer to the source of their being. The moan, the shout, and the rhythmic bodily responses to prayers, song, and sermon are artistic projections of the pain and joy experienced in the struggle of freedom. It is the ability of Black people to express the tragic side of social existence but also their refusal to be imprisoned by its limitations.[29]

Cone supplies a spiritual to illustrate this moment of contextualization and transformation.

> Who found me when I was lost?
> Who helped me to bear my heavy cross?
> Who fixed me up, turned me 'round,
> Left my feet on solid ground?
> I know it was Jesus!
> I know it was the Lord!

A functional Christology shows its worth by "fixing" the suffering, even lifting it, if only for the span of a worship service. To be sure, grim realities await the believer eventually when the "fix" will be tested. Again and again, the cycle will need to be repeated.

Another possible way that a functional Christology might respond to groaning is to see it as intrinsic to the consequences of the kind of life a freedom fighter must live. Cone refers to this way of understanding groaning as he develops the notion of the double life of the freedom fighter.

> The struggle for freedom is God's struggle so the black person in struggle for freedom is the redeemed sinner. The redeemed sinner recognizes that despite his participation in it, the world is unjust, and he must be committed to its liberation. The unredeemed sinner believes that the world is in good hands, and he enjoys

29. Cone, *God of the Oppressed*, 22. See also Bailey, "The Lament Traditions."

his participation in it. Thus the hope for the creation of a new society for all is dependent upon those people who know that struggle is the primary means by which a new age will be inaugurated. . . . It will be changed by the victims whose participation in the present system is against their will. Indeed, while they are percolating in it involuntarily, *voluntarily* they are preparing for its destruction. They are living double lives, one part of which they are seeking to destroy because it contradicts the true self that is being made anew in struggle. Every sensitive black person knows what this means, and it is the source both of our being and not-being. . . . It is this burden that made our ancestors create songs of sorrow and joy.[30]

Cone paraphrases the gospel song "I've Heard of a City Called Heaven" to suggest how the groaning of the double life is engaged in worship. "We know that 'sometimes [we are] tossed and driven,' and 'sometimes [we] don't know where to roam.' But we've 'heard of a city' where 'Jesus is the King' and we are struggling 'to make it [our] home.'"[31] Significantly in the contextualizing of groaning, there is no appeal to a Christology adequate to receive the groaning. Groaning is simply the burden intrinsic to living the liminality of the double life as a clandestine overthrower of oppressive reality. The "transformative moment" is supplied by the news of an eschatological "home," which more and more occupies the attention of one who is "tossed and driven." Jesus functions as the one who secures the heavenly home that shines its light on the upturned face of the beleaguered freedom fighter.

30. Cone, *God of the Oppressed*, 220. As background see Du Bois's explanation of the double consciousness in Black religious life as being caught in the double aim: the simultaneous rejection of American life and the desire to be included in it. *The Souls of Black Folk*, 502; cited in Glaude, *An Uncommon Faith*, 45.

31. Cone, *God of the Oppressed*, 219–20. The official lyrics are:
Sometimes I am tossed and driven, Lord,
Sometimes I don't know where to roam.
I've heard of a city called heaven.
I've started to make it my home.

By the first option, using worship to offload suffering results in episodic creations of a momentary sense of relief. This fleeting sense of relief on the one hand belies the underlying continuous fabric of vexation and provocation, and, on the other hand shreds any confidence in the genuine staying power of the relief itself. This in itself will give rise to questions of theodicy and satisfactory performance.

By the second option, fixating on one's future heavenly home amounts to an escapist orientation. It signals a determination that present reality is hopeless of any resolution, that any expectation of renewal within flawed institutions is impossible. One simply clings in faith to Jesus as the figure who secures the heavenly home for the struggling believer.

In sum, a functional Christology has two practical effects. Either it can shift the burden of groaning by vectoring it away from the groaning one to lodging it in God's act in Christ who has overcome groaning in the resurrection. Or the resurrected Jesus is seen as backstopping the certitude of a new, better home, thereby drawing attention more and more to that future home in order to render the groaning one's ambiguous situation palatable. What is common to each option is that groaning is not embraced, in and of itself, as a way into Jesus.

Cone is aware of the hesitancy that resides within his position to risk this embrace. He uses Søren Kierkegaard's *The Sickness unto Death* as a foil with which to express this reluctance. "Unlike Kierkegaard . . . blacks often refused to go down into that 'loathsome void,' that 'torment of despair,' where one 'struggles with death but cannot die.'"[32] No matter the contradictions they sensed between God's care for them and their continued suffering, "they kept on believing and hoping that 'a change is gonna come'; that trouble would not sink them into permanent despair—what Kierkegaard described as 'not willing to be oneself' or even 'a self,' or lowest of all in despair at willing to be another than himself.' When people do not want to be themselves, but somebody else, that is

32. Cone, *The Cross and the Lynching Tree*, 20, citing "The Sickness unto Death," 341–44.

utter despair."[33] Consequently, Cone's reluctance to follow the way of Kierkegaard blocks access to that strange transcendence that comes from being within the field of eschatological possibilities that is on offer within the crucified Jesus. It is not on offer because of this reluctance to plumb the depths of despair in the company of the One who was abandoned by God; as Cone states, "They did not transcend 'hard living' but faced it head-on, refusing to be silent in the midst of adversity."[34]

Cone's reluctance to read Black groaning from a Kierkegaardian perspective is perhaps made more understandable by white theologian and activist James Perkinson. He emphasizes how the comfortable Danish Christianity of the nineteenth century against which the Dane railed differs strongly from the terrors of the modern American ghetto.[35] However it is not only the contrasting contexts that render Kierkegaard problematic for Black theology. Perkinson thinks the fundamental pathway to consciousness laid out by Kierkegaard is apprehended in the opposite way by Blacks who are terrorized by racism. He explains: For Kierkegaard a "merely ethical life is defined as cozy choice-making, where moral meaning was erected out of the interminable range of possibilities of the sophisticate aesthete who . . . had merely gathered infinity in his head like a whispering chorus of dreams."

However, Kierkegaard insists that this stage must be confronted by an overwhelming demand of divinity that flings this comfortable persona into the great abyss of nothingness defined as the terror-filled recognition of the person's inability to measure up to the demand of divinity. The certain destruction of consciousness however is conditioned by a fully self-conscious entrustment in divinity's forgiveness for one's impossible register of guilt. This final stage vaults commonsense Christianity into the uncertainly of real passion and commitment. It is important to recognize that this pathway to consciousness must be traversed repeatedly

33. Cone, *The Cross and the Lynching Tree*, 20, citing "The Sickness unto Death," 353.

34. Cone, *The Cross and the Lynching Tree*, 20.

35. Perkinson, "Illin' the Evil."

because this consciousness founded in forgiveness is ephemeral. One has this consciousness by not having it.[36] Consciousness is ironic.

Perkinson argues that the inverse path defines the experience of Blacks. Whereas the *final resting point* for Kierkegaard is the ever-repeating vaporizing of the ethical self under the terror of an unrelenting and guilt-producing divine demand, for Blacks this vaporizing of self occurs under the terrorizing dominance of white supremacy and is *the starting point* in their battle for consciousness/dignity. He explains:

> Black theology, on the other hand, *begins* with a terror that is social—inscribed into not just tortured psyche, but living flesh, whether remembered in an ancestor or suffered as one's own. Subjectivity in the historic communities "Blackened" under White supremacy's ruthless hand . . . is, first of all, circumscribed in an opaque and violent *numinosity*, not the alluring aesthetics of a comfortable chamber that is the bourgeoise's "immediate surround." . . . A *Black* Kierkegaardian mapping of life stages might well work in the inverse direction from SK's own bourgeois version—that is *from* the religious through the ethical *to* the aesthetic, a labored exorcism of spirit from the lacerating thickets of White supremacy, by way of political choices mediated in an ever proliferating and novel artistry of "hiding in plain view."[37]

This reconfiguration is founded on the very circumstance Cone reports Blacks' unwillingness to experience "that 'loathsome void,' that 'torment of despair,' where one 'struggles with death but cannot die.'"

For the exorcism of the Black spirit from white supremacy a Black aesthetic is created that comes in both sacred and secular forms. Perkinson cites "the ritual work of the Black church as a re-working the energies of terror into the vitalities of a

---

36. Perkinson, "Illin' the Evil," 360.
37. Perkinson, "Illin' the Evil," 362.

spirited encounter with a God who remains both 'fascinating and terrifying.'"[38] He goes on to say:

> Here is a slave people tethered to the visual surface of their being (skin color), improvising freedom under spiritual auspices, a segregated folk laboring the public order of lynching into a funk order of living-in-spite-of, a ghetto brood "breaking" concrete walls of constraint into jazz rolls and rap ripostes—none of which offers utopian hopes for a radically different polity, but all of which divulge hard-won intuitions of a different way of being human.[39]

Hip-hop emerges for Perkinson as an effective aesthetic through its use of grotesquery to include the very thing it rejects "in such a way that both the comic *and* the tragic, the absurd *and* the sincere, the morbid *and* the manic, are made to appear without canceling each other out, but also without negating the edge of protest."[40] In that sense hip-hop participates in Kierkegaardian irony. It "grants hope by honestly posturing [its] own lack of hope."[41] Perkinson thinks that the theological backstop for hip-hop is Kierkegaard's construction of Christology. He lays out the irony fundamental to this Christology.

> Christ is the supreme conjunction of infinity-in-the-finite, as Absolute Paradox. The epitome of the contra-dictory ideality that is consciousness. . . . Not only must Jesus himself be indirectly embraced as a master of irony precisely in his claim "I am God," but his very constitu-tion as the God-Human embodies the greatest possible qualitative contradiction.[42]

---

38. Perkinson, "Illin' the Evil," 363.

39. Perkinson, "Illin' the Evil," 357. See Glaude's use of an "as yet" sensibil-ity: open-ended, tentative, unsure, performance-driven, and unsurprised by failure to characterize his construction of an "uncommon faith."

40. Perkinson, "Illin' the Evil," 371.

41. Perkinson, "Illin' the Evil," 375.

42. Perkinson, "Illin' the Evil," 368.

> Hip-hop trickery is a pop culture text of resurrection, a
> form of street idiom positioned against hopelessness and
> death. [It] grants hope by honestly posturing [its] own
> lack of hope.[43]

Bringing this section to a close, this book maintains that when Christology is reduced to technique or aesthetic, no matter how understandable and creative, groaning and the burden it carries cannot be adequately encompassed. What we argue for is a Christology that takes seriously the mystery of the resurrection of a crucified, broken body that becomes the reigning metaphor of the presence of Christ in the church and in the world. Christ turns his mangled body toward a mangled world. He is an active sufferer with all the despised and deplored. The resurrection makes his wounds ever fresh for the sake of those who suffer to accompany them in their suffering. Because by his cross he draws all persons to himself, the promise of new creation guaranteed by his resurrected body cannot be the exclusive right of any particular group. As his wounds make him open to all suffering, so his resurrection makes his death-defying life possible within his wounds. This mystery of the power of a resurrected-crucified Christ to embrace and transform the burden of groaning is well captured in a prayer included in a collection of Black folklore:

> You heard me when I laid at hell's dark door
> With no weapon in my hand
> And no God in my heart,
> And I cried for three long days and nights.
> You heard me, Lawd,
> And stooped so low
> And snatched me from the hell
> Of eternal death and damnation.
> You cut loose my stammerin' tongue,
> You established my feet on the rock of Salvation
> And yo' voice was heard in the rumblin' judgment.[44]

43. Perkinson, "Illin' the Evil," 375.

44. Cited in Hurston, *Mules and Men*, 44.

Today Black congregations in this country do not worship under conditions of chattel slavery and the terror of lynching. However, the contemporary groaning we have documented carries the freight of the physical, mental, emotional, and spiritual aggression under which Black people continue to suffer. Singing melds this suffering with the story of God's presence in the world in the figure of the resurrected-crucified Jesus. Worship becomes a place where not only singers can express out of their own suffering a sympathy and empathy with what Jesus endured, but as importantly, the worshipper is assured that Jesus knows the depth of their sufferings because of his continuous presence as the crucified one brought back from the dead. He is the witness who welcomes hurt.

> Nobody knows the trouble I've seen,
> Nobody knows but Jesus . . .
> Glory Hallelujah!

This intimate mutual sharing of personal suffering with the story of Jesus' suffering is the key to the movement into the transformative moment. This is the moment where Jesus' victory in the resurrection is applied to those who know he joins them in their groaning. Since Jesus has conquered all manner of evil and the curse of death, no systemic oppression has power to prevent Jesus' sharing his victory through the Holy Spirit with the oppressed. Clinging to the resurrected-crucified Jesus, the one who groans always has the hope of liberation. It is possible to resist oppression and fight for freedom with stamina and verve.

A universalizing sweep attaches both to the oppression borne by Christ, and to his victory. The death of the Son of Man cuts the ground from under any special human pleading; his resurrection takes away from anyone's hands the specification of what that victory must be. Those who stand under the cross become the community that affirms the diversity and genuineness of human suffering in Christ—the chorus of groaning. It is this same community to whom Christ gives the panoply of eschatological possibilities for something new to spring up that "no eye has seen, nor ear heard, nor the human heart conceived" (1 Cor 2:9; Isa 64:4).

The questions posed by Cone and Evans as they grapple with how the Christian message is shaped to respond to the perduring wreckage of racism continue their challenge. Our investigation turns now to the work of a new generation of Black religious thinkers, Eddie Glaude Jr. and M. Shawn Copeland.

Chapter 6

BLACK THEOLOGY AS A CONTEXT FOR TRANSFORMING GROANING—II

Eddie S. Glaude Jr. and M. Shawn Copeland

An Uncommon Faith

Eddie Glaude, whose reaction to the death of George Floyd we noted earlier in laying the landscape of groaning, rejects treating groaning either as something to be vectored onto Jesus or something to endure by concentrating on our heavenly home. Glaude is a professor of religion and African American studies at Princeton University. His academic work is informed significantly by his reading of James Baldwin and nineteenth-century American writers.

Glaude struggles to keep the burden of his suffering and his advocacy for social justice more consciously grounded in a matrix of new life springing out of ongoing wounds. We are calling this construal of the matrix "cruciform," however this does not necessarily imply christological underpinning. In fact, as will become clear, Glaude will develop this model in a thoroughgoing secular way. Even so, this cruciform matrix provides fertile ground for his burden to be contextualized and transformed.

Our plan is first to review how Glaude works with this matrix in a more popular setting through essays and interviews that occur before and after the death of Floyd. We will show him using this matrix to render three new possibilities that promise renewal. These are, in turn, (1) the embracing of grief in hope, which issues in the enunciation of a new determination to serve a vision, (2) the embracing of death as shared loss, which produces the catalysts of radical community and equality, and (3) the inescapable requirement of confession as the womb out of which one can move from the finality of national death into the birth again of national possibility. We will then proceed to locate these possibilities within the broad sweep of Glaude's more scholarly presentation of his position.

Embracing Grief in Hope

In a radio interview on Detroit's WDET November 20, 2020, with Stephen Henderson, the memory of the trauma of the summer of George Floyd remained fresh and raw.[1] Glaude spoke candidly and openly. He lamented the overwhelming mountain of epistemic ignorance among white people, of their not being interested in knowing, of willful ignorance. "Is this America?" Glaude asks. "White racism is a reality people are not programmed to see. They are socialized to be awful." He hears himself screaming at the top of his lungs and sees no progress. Exhaustion drives him to tears. He asks, "Will racism and disease finally choke the life out of this fragile experiment in democracy?"[2]

In his struggles with fatigue, doubt, rage, and sorrow, Glaude testifies to the power of the Black gospel song "Precious Lord, Take My Hand."[3] Written in 1933 by Thomas A. Dorsey as an outpouring of his sorrow, living through the deaths of his wife and their newborn son, this most popular Black gospel song became the means to channel both Glaude's grief and his hope. The intimacy and assurance in this gospel song, sung in a situation of dire threat,

1. I am paraphrasing and summarizing this hour-long interview.
2. Glaude, "We Cannot Wait," 25.
3. Found in *Glory to God*, 834.

embraced Glaude at his wit's end with a measure of support that he received at a deep level.

What emerged from the meeting of his grief and the spiritual was Glaude's voicing his dream of setting white people free from being white.[4] Thus, this is an example of him employing the cruciform matrix. He spoke of the need to deconstruct the structure of white supremacy, which he asserts is based on a lie, established at the founding of America, that slaves were not human beings.[5] The deconstruction of this reigning lie is a program entered into consciously, deliberately, with the intention of reimagining oneself, moving from living within a discredited myth of exceptionalism[6] to living within a new aspirational myth of justice.

4. In "We Cannot Wait," 25, Glaude writes that the future of American democracy depends, in part, "on white America's willingness to leave the shibboleths of American racism behind—to give up this insidious belief that because they are white they ought to be valued more than others." However, he adds the proviso, "But we cannot wait on them. Those of us who will dare to actually learn from our history must figure out how to be together differently in a New America."

5. In a PBS interview with Walter Isaacson, September 15, 2020 ("Princeton Prof. on Race Relations"), Glaude expands upon his notion of the "lie." "Well, the lie is this belief that we're the shining city on the hill, the redeemer nation, an example of democracy achieved. And we tell the lie in order to hide and obscure what we have actually done. [James] Baldwin writes, in 1964, in this essay entitled 'The White Problem,' he says, there's a fatal flaw at the beginning of the country. And I'm paraphrasing here. He says, there's a fatal flaw at the beginning of the country, because these Christians who decided they were going to build a democracy also decided to have slaves. And in order to justify the role of these chattel, they had to say that they were not human beings, because, if they were not human beings, then no crime would have been committed. And then Baldwin writes this line, which is at the heart of the book. That lie is at the heart of our present problem. So, the lie we have told about Black people and their capacity, the lie we have told about white people and their superiority, the lies we tell about what we have done in the name of that superiority, all of that, in some ways, is the scaffolding that protects our supposed innocence. And as Baldwin says in 'The Fire Next Time,' the innocence is the crime, right? The innocence is the crime."

6. Jake Sullivan reexamines the ideology of American exceptionalism in "Yes, America Can Still Lead the World." While arguing convincingly for a resumption of American leadership in the world on the basis of the founding of this nation on a set of ideas rather than ethnicity, he does not address the

We must be careful to note, again, that any christological motivations for Glaude's reaching for this spiritual in his situation of extremity are ambiguous. In fact, as we continue to explore his use of the cruciform model, it will become clear that he affirms the option of employing religious resources in a non-metaphysical way.[7]

Shared Loss Becoming Radical Community and Equality

Glaude's essays in national publications provide him an outlet for sharing with a wide readership his struggle to find hope for a nation within the grip of historic grim realities. Reading through his pieces reveals him taking an unflinching immersion into groaning as a national womb. Within the womb of groaning, radical community and equality emerge as catalysts. An essay, "The Pandemic Will Pass. Our Grief Will Endure," is illustrative of the catalytic effect of the community and equality that issue from this womb. Written just as the outlines of the enormity of the pandemic's devastation were emerging, Glaude has the opportunity to reflect on his listening to a chorus of groaning. The actual reality of the disruption of families and shredding of communities has crushed early predictions, which only gives searing urgency to Glaude's insistence, "Those who survive this madness will have to figure out how to live together in the company of grief."[8]

Glaude recognizes that rituals of grieving allow us to place grief in a context of meaning, which provides an avenue for making sense out of what is happening to us. Cruelly, the pandemic prevents this company of grief from coming together. "We are siloed, segregated and left to our own devices—all of which intensifies the

---

revision of that exceptionalism with respect to the systemic flaws of white racism that were present from the start of America's national expansion. For more on the influence of education in the classics on America's founding, see Poser, "He Wants to Save Classics from Whiteness."

7. Glaude, *Uncommon Faith*, 47, where he writes of using "religious stories to the very task of self-creation that struggles against concrete social and political realities."

8. Glaude, "The Pandemic Will Pass."

depth of grief in the face of mass death."[9] This compounds present groaning over loss by adding to it a load of regret over not being able to say good-bye properly. With telling effect, Glaude observes, "This sense of regret will cling to [our] grief, giving it jagged edges that repeatedly cut and wound."[10]

Against a strong presumption that we are left to our own devices to deal with death, Glaude says that what can grow within that womb of unimaginable grief is an overpowering sense of shared relatedness with the dead. The universality of the pandemic's victims makes inescapable the realization that "no matter the color of their skin, the people they loved, their Zip code, the language they spoke, or the political party they supported—they are *ours*."[11]

Thus, community and equality become for Glaude catalytic for new initiatives. Glaude sees emerging out of that universe of shared relatedness in mass death a new chance for national unity. Public rituals acknowledging collective sorrow will give long-term focus to our nation's facing mass death. Glaude imagines a spectrum of occasions such as: national days of mourning and prayer, a public reading of the names of those who have died, memorials commemorating the lives of those who died on the front lines of saving lives, and honoring the global effort to develop and distribute a vaccine. He projects that growing within the womb of grief is "the act of living [differently] all through."[12] Rabid partisanship, crass individualism and breathtaking inequality will give way to a new sense of connection and bond.

Glaude wrote for a national publication. However, it is possible to place his thoughts squarely inside of the cruciform model of contextualization and transformation we are presenting. This essay written for a general audience draws from Glaude's study of the "uncommon faith" of W. E. B. Du Bois, which we will review later in this chapter.

9. Glaude, "The Pandemic Will Pass."

10. Glaude, "The Pandemic Will Pass."

11. Glaude, "The Pandemic Will Pass."

12. Glaude quotes C. S. Lewis from *A Grief Observed*.

Confession as the Pathway to Empowerment

Glaude's essay on the pandemic was written in April 2020, before the brutal murder of George Floyd injected fresh trauma into the nation's psyche. We have already reviewed publications of Glaude's visceral reaction of groaning in May and June as he grappled with the implications of this and other appalling instances of police brutality. An essay in *Time* magazine in July 2020 allows him an opportunity to view these events from a perspective of national history. Glaude's reflections are drawn from the history of the betrayal of Black aspirations in the era of Ronald Reagan as this is chronicled in the writing of James Baldwin. Again, our interest is in understanding how Glaude thinks through this trauma as he is guided by the cruciform model and the way he expresses the implications of this model in language that could be received by a wide and diverse readership.

The video of George Floyd dying "combined with the vulnerability caused by COVID-19 and the feeling that the country is broken bring[s] us all to the brink of madness and, apparently, to the precipice of significant change."[13] Glaude calls this an "odd admixture"—madness and a moment of possibility—making urgent the question: What turns the instability of madness into the foundation for renewal? Guided by Baldwin's documentary film *I Heard It through the Grapevine*, which captures his trip through the South on the eve of the election of Reagan in 1980, Glaude points to the indispensable component of confession as the only way for whites to get past the seemingly ineradicable inability to change. Glaude quotes Baldwin, "They have never confessed their crimes, and they don't know how to confess their crimes. . . . If you can't confess, you can't be forgiven, and if you can't be forgiven, you can't get past it. That is the sin against the Holy Ghost. . . . The only way to get past it is to confess."[14]

Significant is Glaude's choice to mention Baldwin's bringing up the trope of the unforgivable sin of blasphemy against the Holy

13. Glaude, "The Country That Refused to Change," 82.
14. Glaude, "The Country That Refused to Change," 85.

Spirit (Matt 12:32; Mark 3:28–30; Luke 12:10). While interpreters are not of one mind as to the precise meaning of this, what seems clear from the texts is that it is an act of utter rebellion against God by denying God as the doer of God's own acts. Even though each gospel sets the statement in a unique context, the sense of finality to the consequences of denial is common to the citations. Glaude seizes upon that sense of finality as coloring our national failure, but poses the possibility of overcoming that finality through confessing "the ugliness of who we are as nation. . . . We cannot stick our heads back in the sand or seek comfort in our national illusions or our so-called innocence. This moral reckoning requires confession and repair. If we fail this time, and it may well be our last chance, ours will be the latest addition to the ruins."[15]

In this essay Glaude makes use of a secularized version of the cruciform model to contextualize and transform the burden of groaning in a way that is both honest and bracing. His language shows him working on the idea that transformative good can issue forth from the abyss of madness. He is clearly reaching out to white readers to urge us to undertake a fundamental religious practice: confession and repair. Glaude holds out his hope that "we now have a chance to choose a new America," that the motivating ideals are ready to empower our transformation, but only as we, as a country, undertake the disciplines of confession and repair.

A Chastened, Pragmatic Religious Naturalism

Glaude's more popular writings and presentations have their roots in his work as a scholar of African American religion and American studies. In order to gain a fuller appreciation of his influential voice we will examine two examples of his thinking. One is a 2019 scholarly article where Glaude describes reading Walt Whitman's *Democratic Vistas* (1871) in conversation with James Baldwin's *No Name in the Street* (1972).[16] The other is Glaude's book setting out

15. Glaude, "The Country That Refused to Change," 85.
16. Glaude, "The Magician's Serpent."

an "uncommon faith," which is inspired by the writings of W. E. B. Du Bois.[17]

i. Confession Giving Birth to Freedom from Illusion: Walt Whitman and James Baldwin

In "The Magician's Serpent: Race and the Tragedy of American Democracy" Glaude begins with Walt Whitman's plea in *Democratic Vistas* as he saw the victory of the ideals of the Civil War deteriorate after the war into a contest for greed and suppression:

> Whitman pined for an overarching narrative that went beyond mere liberal proceduralism. Something more fundamental, that transcended or, better, transformed the mundane into a more "religious" quality, was needed if the nation was to be otherwise. He yearned for a kind of consensus rooted in a spiritualized democratic individuality that bound one to the other. But the country fell short. Out of the ashes of the Civil War emerged a nation bustling with the energy of commerce, "endowed with a vast and more and more appointed body," he wrote, but "with little or no soul."[18] For Whitman, it was not enough that the country be held together by a new politics; instead, "original poets" were needed, persons who would mount "the horizon like planets, stars of the first magnitude . . ." and "give more compaction and more moral identity to these states."[19] Heroic in, perhaps, Thomas Carlyle's sense of the word, these "original poets" would address the hollowness at the heart of the country.[20]

Reflecting on Whitman's "spiritualized democratic individuality," Glaude writes:

---

17. Glaude, *An Uncommon Faith.*

18. Whitman, *Democratic Vistas*, 326.

19. Whitman, *Democratic Vistas*, 323.

20. Glaude, "The Magician's Serpent," 11. One thinks of "The Hill We Must Climb," the poem Amanda Gorman spoke at the inauguration of President Joseph R. Biden on January 20, 2021.

I turn to Whitman's apocalyptic fervor in these Trumpian times, to his condemnation of avarice, his horror over the fraying fabric of the nation, and his call for a different kind of individuality. His idea of individuality is rooted in an understanding of self-reliance that involves, at its best, an attentiveness to the quality of others' lives in order to secure the conditions for our fellows' flourishing as a feature of our own, and to those poets who would give us a literature that speaks to "the common people, the life-blood of democracy" and who guide us down a different path to a more excellent way of being in the world.[21]

Glaude finds potential in Whitman's theme of the common people as the lifeblood of democracy and expands upon it with more from *Democratic Vistas*. "To work in, if we may so term it, and justify God, His divine aggregate, the People—this, I say, is what democracy is for; and this is what our America means, and is doing—may I not say, has done? If not, she means nothing more, and does nothing more, than any other land."[22]

Yet, Glaude points out, "in 1874, just three years after the publication of *Democratic Vistas*, in 'A Hint to Preachers and Authors,' Whitman wrote: 'As if we had not strained the voting and digestive caliber of American Democracy to the utmost for the last fifty years with the millions of ignorant foreigners, we have infused a powerful percentage of Blacks, with about as much intellect and caliber (in the mass) as so many baboons."[23] Glaude observes that Whitman's

commitment to the belief that white people matter more than others[24] . . . [makes him fail] to be the kind of per-

21. Glaude, "The Magician's Serpent," 11. Whitman, *Democratic Vistas*, 388.

22. Glaude, "The Magician's Serpent," 15, citing Whitman, *Democratic Vistas*, 338.

23. Glaude, "The Magician's Serpent," 12. The passage is found in Whitman, *Prose Work, 1892*, cited in Outka, "Whitman and Race," 296.

24. Glaude, "The Magician's Serpent," 13. See further Glaude, *Democracy in Black*.

son his view of democracy demands. . . . That perception or, better, choice gets in the way of his embrace of
democratic virtue [the ethical demand to be attentive to
the quality of others' lives, that sense of responsibility to
our fellows, in our effort to be more self-reliant]. It limits
his capacity for generosity, his sense of humility, and his
idea of benevolence and mutuality. In short, it limits his
view of justice.[25]

Glaude presents James Baldwin a century later using Whitman as a guide in coming to grips with the betrayal of the Civil
Rights Movement sealed by the triple assassinations of Medgar
Evers, Malcolm X, and Martin Luther King Jr. coupled with the
election of Ronald Reagan as president. Glaude sees Baldwin making use of the cruciform matrix. Within what Baldwin sees as the
rubble of the democratic life, he continues to hold up the belief
that "America's greatness rests with its willingness to finally embrace the ideal of who and what it is,"[26] so eloquently expressed
by Whitman. But this can come about only as America is able and
willing to conduct a reckoning with the dark history of this country. Failing that reckoning, the only choice is to repeat the illusion
that this is a white nation and to ignite violence when that illusion
is threatened. This is why taking responsibility, performing the
discipline of confession, is the only pathway to freeing one's self
of the illusion, the serpent that eats all others. This discipline of
confession will require tremendous spiritual resources and on the
outcome of that reckoning the future of democracy depends.[27]

This essay is notable for the creative way Glaude presents a
conversation between speakers over a century apart. His scholarly
work grounds his own voice in the national conversation as he
implores us to avoid repeating the willful national forgetfulness of
slavery and to take up the risk of repair that is anchored in confession. Confession belongs in the mainstream of religious behavior,
and it is a risky practice because a destruction of one's self may be

25. Glaude, "The Magician's Serpent," 13.

26. Glaude, "The Magician's Serpent," 19.

27. Glaude, "The Magician's Serpent," 20.

required. Yet, as Glaude rightly presents Baldwin, nothing better can come to life outside of the womb of confession.

ii. A Hope Not Hopeless but Unhopeful: W. E. B. Du Bois

To review, as we have listened to Eddie Glaude's sensitive, deeply probing, and historically rooted grappling with America's racial burden, we have several times noted how he urges us to see the possibility of renewal emerging out of perilous contexts. Our term for describing his path of thinking is *cruciform*. Cruciform, as we have stated, is the process of the emergence of something life-giving out of a womb of death. We have advanced the argument that Glaude has used the cruciform matrix for contextualizing and transforming his profound wrestling with America's curse of racism. In his work *An Uncommon Faith* he presents the outlines of a systematic description of the cruciform model of contextualization and transformation. He develops this in his study of African American religion as formulated by W. E. B. Du Bois.

Central, for Glaude, to the religious impulse is the cry for Help! Help! This is due to his own "intimate relationship with loss and because of the fact—and it is a disconcerting fact indeed—that the people to whom I belong, not just my immediate family but those who were snatched from the shores of distant lands, have had to grapple with loss as a background condition for their efforts at self-creation, and as a fundamental feature of their sojourn in this nation." Glaude feels the religious impulse most keenly as "that sense of helplessness in the face of uncertainty and loss (especially in light of violence) and the broken fragments left in its wake."[28] This is the context that produces groaning.

In the face of groaning, intelligence, however passionate and critical, only takes us so far. Glaude shares from Du Bois's *The Souls of Black Folk*: "The bowed and bent old man cries, with thrice re-peated wail: 'O Lord, keep me from sinking down,' and he rebukes

---

28. Glaude, *An Uncommon Faith*, 43.

the devil of doubt who can whisper: 'Jesus is dead and God's gone away.' Yet the soul hunger is there, the restlessness of the savage, the wail of the wanderer, and the plaint is put in one little phrase, *'My soul wants something that's new, that's new.'*"[29] Again, Glaude appeals to Du Bois's moving formulation of "the deep religious feeling of the real negro heart":

> the stirring, unguided might of powerful human souls who have lost the guiding star of the past and are seeking in the great night a new religious ideal. Some day the Awakening will come when the pent-up vigor of ten million souls shall sweep irresistibly toward the Goal, out of the Valley of the Shadow of Death, where all that makes life worth living—Liberty, Justice, and Right—is marked "For White People Only."[30]

In this present state of affairs, Glaude, influenced by Du Bois's unflinching appraisal of life in America, posits for Black people "an uncommon faith" of a "chastened pragmatic religious naturalism."[31] This faith has three legs: (1) *Meliorism*, defined as recognizing that the world is uncertain, that "it can be saved or it can go to hell, depending on our choices, actions, and efforts." (2) The *embracing of ambiguity and uncertainty.* "The open-ended character of experience does not offer clear pathways to achieve desired ends. This makes the struggle for Black freedom all the more perilous and demands a different kind of grounding for the strenuous mood." (3) *A natural piety rooted in commitment to generations to come*, a commitment pursued against the headwinds of loneliness and despair.[32] We will explore each of these supports.

Meliorism is grounded in a belief of steady improvement, which generates a basic hopefulness to living. Glaude's pragmatic experience with the struggle for racial justice does not allow him

29. Glaude, *An Uncommon Faith*, 48; quoting from Du Bois, *The Souls of Black Folk*, 542.

30. Glaude, *An Uncommon Faith*, 45–46; quoting from Du Bois, *The Souls of Black Folk*, 505.

31. Glaude, *An Uncommon Faith*, 46.

32. Glaude, *An Uncommon Faith*, 48.

that confidence. He does not abandon a stance of hope; however, he gives that stance greater nuance in light of his experience. An uncommon faith will support a "hope not hopeless, but unhopeful,"[33] a phrase he borrows from Du Bois. What does this provocative construction mean?

Glaude is careful to note that the warrant for this hope is not lodged in the realm of the metaphysical. While neither Du Bois nor Glaude set aside the metaphysical, functionally it does not play a determinative role in anchoring hope. "I hope and on such claim to authority as only we alone, in our uncertainty, can bring to it."[34] Glaude expands on this point: Hope is "rooted in a world of action that all too often frustrates our aims and ends. We nevertheless muster the courage to act with little to no guarantee that these actions will secure our desired aims and end. We do so because, in the end, it is all up to us."[35] This is a pragmatic, performance-based meliorism.

But who is the "us" that gives warrant to such hope? Glaude asks. He has previously referenced descriptors as: "the real negro heart," "the stirring unguided might of powerful human souls," and "the world of action." Becoming more specific, he observes that "this world can dirty you on the inside so bad that you don't like yourself anymore,"[36] and this outrage upon "the real negro heart" has the power to overdetermine "the conditions within which we act, the very conditions that shape our striving for better selves."[37] Yet, in the face of all that, in the end, it is all up to us. This arduous seeking requires a kind of love and trust of self that is deliberate, dogged, and single-minded.

33. Glaude, *An Uncommon Faith*, 48; quoting from Du Bois, *The Souls of Black Folk*, 507.

34. Glaude, *An Uncommon Faith*, 49, takes this phrase from Cavell, "Hope Against Hope," 182.

35. Glaude, *An Uncommon Faith*, 48; quoting from Du Bois, *The Souls of Black Folk*, 507.

36. Glaude, *An Uncommon Faith*, 49. Glaude alludes to Toni Morrison's *Beloved*.

37. Glaude, *An Uncommon Faith*, 49.

What emerges is a hope not hopeless but unhopeful. The actions taken in such a hope are those of broken, wounded souls who seek "a higher self in a world that denies one standing." Their work is made all the more difficult in that Black people have to seek that self "amid the wounds and shards of a personal life, ... the material and psychic conditions that block the way to our understanding of who we can be and what we are capable of."[38] It follows from this kind of hope that such an uncommon faith will be infused with *ambiguity and uncertainty*, which is the second feature of uncommon faith. Because those who struggle for a higher self do so as broken people going up against material and psychic conditions blocking their desires, there are no clear pathways to achieve desired ends. Glaude reminds us: "This makes the struggle for Black freedom all the more perilous and demands a different kind of grounding for the strenuous mood."

This mood is colored by an "as yet" sensibility: open-ended, tentative, unsure, performance-driven, and unsurprised by failure. The striking use of the formula "as yet" may be Glaude's direct response to a formulation of classical Christian eschatology, the "not yet" of the flowering of the new heaven and earth. We will explore the relationship between "as yet" and "not yet" in our reflections on Glaude's position.

A chastened, pragmatic meliorism executed in the mood of "as yet" can be a bleak and daunting basis on which to construct a life. Yet, under Glaude's hands, there is a tenacity, a grittiness, a resiliency to such a program of living. Here is where I detect a secular cruciform matrix, which Glaude uses to contextualize and transform the burden carried by groaning. He employs this matrix in the service of his *fundamental commitment to generations to come*, the final feature of uncommon faith. Fragile, finite, and in some cases, broken selves work for our children and our children's children to secure the values that we have come to cherish.[39]

In sum, an uncommon faith asserts that Black transformation begins with brokenness. "Here one refuses to view wound

38. Glaude, *An Uncommon Faith*, 49.

39. Glaude, *Uncommon Faith*, 53.

and brokenness as a permanent fixed state and aspires instead to something 'more'—where a relentless faith in the possible, without metaphysical guarantees, evidences itself . . . in the service of the world as it *could* be."[40] Ever and again, one picks up the pieces of life which have been relegated to the trash bin and transforms them into that which is beautiful. "At the moment of the transformation a world, a different way of being in the world, is made possible, and it is within this space of brokenness we make ourselves and the world anew."[41] Glaude's secular cruciform matrix claims that the very shards of living will provide a foundation, without the security of comforting illusions, on which to step forward and dare to be, wounds and all. In what is perhaps his most candid formulation he states, "I am suggesting that the aspiration to wholeness is misguided; beauty is found elsewhere in the life we make with the pieces."[42] That is uncommon faith.

"As Yet" and "Not Yet"

Glaude places the burden of concern conveyed by the emotion of weeping within a matrix that bears striking resemblance to the resurrected-crucified Jesus. As such his "as yet" forecast of the future becomes a conversation partner with the "not yet" construal of the future flowering of God's reign in Christian eschatology. The chief difference is that the "not yet" is rooted in living in the confidence of an "even now," a resetting of the terms of living pegged to one's utter trust in the crucified-resurrected Jesus as the bearer and repository of God's kingdom of justice and peace. To conclude our engagement with Glaude's thoughtful, vulnerable, and courageous outline of a natural faith, we will consider certain aspects of this conversation.

40. Glaude, *Uncommon Faith*, 54.

41. Glaude, *Uncommon Faith*, 53–54.

42. Glaude, *Uncommon Faith*, 63n41.

Glaude privileges the African American "soul" in that it bears within it an undying claim to liberty, justice, and right,[43] a claim that has found a way to assert itself constantly in the face of the strongest headwinds of the American lie. This is the "even now" point from which Glaude launches his trajectory of assertion. Groaning, at times, is the medium of that assertion. Groaning is contextualized within the womb of ethnicity and history, and, by an act of sheer will, nourished, perhaps, from religious sources, is transformed into renewed self-love and self-trust. Consequently, the groaner is able to press forward for the sake of coming generations, but always along a path overshadowed by the realistic and pragmatic "as yet."

The "as yet" quality of the future derives its tentativeness and poignancy from the brutal record of white supremacy's dominance that shows little sign of diminishing. The "yet-ness" refers back to the ideal of the full flowering of what resides deep in African American consciousness (*"My soul wants something that's new, that's new"*). Thus, it may be said that the "even now/as yet" dynamic is autochthonous, self-referencing and self-directed.

The christologically funded matrix model we have been using as our baseline confesses that God has established a new home for the contextualization and transformation of groaning within the presence of the resurrected-crucified Jesus. The Jesus who now lives beyond death still carries his open wounds. The wounded Lord is the opening of God to gather us up in our most abject state. The tortured appraisal of "as yet" is welcomed within the womb of Christ's wounds. Within that womb God intends for us, wounded persons, to draw limited, but genuine gifts of new life that flow from the resurrected wounded Lord.

The "even now" of our reconstituting experience comes to us as a gift. This is a carefully nuanced gift. On the one hand, it is quite apart from whatever ideal, self-love, self-trust, or obligation we may have on hand to give us courage. On the other hand, God's gift of new life resonates with the human claim for dignity,

43. This orientation around an African cultural source also informs Evans's elliptical Christology.

by taking that claim into the realm of the "even now." This "even now" is a down payment against the full flowering of what God has in store for us in the person of the resurrected Christ. This experience of the "even now" does not erase the conditions of groaning necessarily. It is designed to allow us to thrive and flourish as new beings in the midst of such conditions, while giving us newfound resources to struggle to experience more of what God has shown us in the new human being of the resurrected Jesus.

Because the "even now" finally does not reside in us, but in God, it is not vulnerable to any human power to dissuade or destroy. This is what changes the "as yet" to "not yet" as a way to characterize the ambiguous and uncertain aspects of our present life. Consequently, while self-love and self-trust are to be expected from the gift of the "even now," love and trust in God is indispensable as the grounds on which to access this gift of the "even now."

M. Shawn Copeland: A Cruciform Transformational Matrix

From her deep roots in Roman Catholic spirituality and theology, M. Shawn Copeland sets out a position that has a striking similarity to the one for which I have been advocating. As a Black Catholic theologian, she struggles to comprehend the unmeasurable dimensions of societal suffering experienced by whomever is reduced to an essential substance that is denigrated.

> In the United States, such essentialization and reduction leaves indigenous peoples, all people of color—irrespective of their societal status, all economically impoverished people—irrespective of their constructed racial designation, including whiteness, all differently abled persons, queer and transgendered persons, Arabs, Muslims, Jews, and all disempowered or powerless social "others" abandoned to societally sanctioned violence and threats of violence.[44]

44. Copeland, *Knowing Christ Crucified*, xxiii.

She points out that "such events of massive public suffering often render its victims powerless or mute, push them to borders of hopelessness or despair," and the self-reporting of groaning we have documented bears this out. Yet, she observes, "despite intense and protracted suffering, many of these children, women, and men confound the sheer horror of their pain, claim agency, seize righteous anger, and struggle against the evil so manifest in cruelty and injustice."[45] She sets out to give an account of how a spirituality centered on the cross of Christ makes this possible.

Her thinking begins by taking up the insight earlier developed by Cone and Evans that Jesus' "suffering showed enslaved people that he understood them and their suffering like no one else."[46] They recognized that he would help them negotiate their world with righteous anger and dignity. She recognizes worship as a powerful setting to meet Jesus and highlights the critical role the singing of spirituals plays in the worshipper's reaching out to Jesus.

A spiritual, she defines "as the moaned or sung utterance of an enslaved woman or man in response to or about a given experience that had communal and/or universal application."[47] Spirituals may begin in groaning. Her insightful analysis of the construction of a spiritual allows us to appreciate its power.

The power of the spirituals derives from the artistic employment of four components: the anamnetic, midrashic, charismatic, and apocalyptic. The *anamnetic* component of the spiritual holds in memory the scattered and forgotten ancestors. It allows the singer to escape the despair of loneliness and to be embraced within the broad stream of his or her people. The spiritual's *midrashic* mode of composition can be traced as the spiritual reshapes, retells, and conflates biblical material so that the spiritual tells anew of the mercy of God and the place of Jesus as friend. The *charismatic* feature comes through the risk of singing "of the power of the Spirit to bring life out of death and despair, to bring health and wholeness out of pain, to pour joy into broken hearts." Finally, the

---

45. Copeland, *Knowing Christ Crucified*, xix.

46. Copeland, *Knowing Christ Crucified*, 26.

47. This paragraph is drawn from Copeland, *Knowing Christ Crucified*, 44.

apocalyptic thrust of the song takes the stories of women and men who risk singing of the Spirit's power and weaves those stories into the liberating promises of the merciful reign of God.

In the spiritual "Were You There When They Crucified My Lord?" all four components are present. The intent of the spiritual is to trace, step by step, the narrative of the crucifixion and resurrection of Jesus, the pivotal moment of Christology. The midrashic composition draws features from the four distinct Gospel accounts. Indeed, the spiritual is elastic in that the singer can include all or only some of these events. The repeated question that haunts the spiritual "Were You There?" brings anamnetic lights to the singing by invoking the shared bond of suffering of slaves with Jesus from the time of the Middle Passage to the microaggressions of the present. Yes, we were/are there with him, and yes, he was/is there with us. The charismatic power comes from this awareness of one's personal suffering being embraced in his story of his cross. However, the power derived from this identification is only sustainable by the final question, "Were you there when the stone was rolled away?" This is the all-important apocalyptic thrust of the resurrection which the singer calls out as marking the intrusion of an entirely new liberating reign of God. Yes, I am there.

Worship renders the foretaste of this reign in palpable ways. It "causes me to tremble, tremble, tremble." Worship becomes the place where suffering is contextualized within the narrative—which is sung, preached, and prayed—of Jesus's cross and resurrection. In that matrix, transformation of the one who groans happens. "We find traces of his cross in the singing of indigenous peoples in the midst of disregard and neglect; in defiant dances of fiesta in the midst of doubt and fear."[48]

Copeland is keenly aware that transformation happens within the Christian's dialectical relationship to the resurrected-crucified Jesus. She asserts: "The Crucified One must be embraced if the Resurrected One is to be recognized."[49] She insists that Christians only have access to the eschatological power of the resurrected

48. Copeland, *Knowing Christ Crucified*, xxiii.

49. Copeland, *Knowing Christ Crucified*, 154.

Christ as they yield their pain to the ongoing vulnerability of Jesus. She describes this new state of being as "new life breaking through, formally and materially, the cosmic, psychic, and moral disorder brought about by the reign of sin."

This dialectical relationship of the Christian is rooted in a deeper dialectical relationship within the resurrected body of the Lord itself. The crucified Jesus is seen in the risen Christ. "If the sight of resurrected Jesus left disciples dazed, they remain gripped by an unshakable certainty that the Jesus of Nazareth who had been crucified was, by the power of the God of Israel, raised from the dead."[50] The stories of his appearances in Emmaus and Jerusalem are characterized by insistent corporeality. Yet, she recognizes that "the body in which Jesus is raised does not belong to this world." The resurrected-crucified Jesus is "a new and different reality and signals a new and different mode of living." The resurrection represents a radical breaking with material reality as we know it. It is a new reality recognized by the heart before it is "grasped by the sense and confirmed by the mind." Thinking has to catch up with feeling.

Finally, Copeland correctly distinguishes resurrection appearances from psychological effects of mere enthusiasm or byproduces of frenzied despair. They are not simply solitary singular inner experiences. Instead, as Paul points out in 1 Corinthians 15, they possess the character of public events and involve groups as well as individuals. As such, they are best construed as transformative events wherein the risen Lord gives insight and direction to communities to embark on extending his mission of liberation in his name. This they are to do against severe opposition from power-structures who resist the liberating news of the gospel. They are to persevere with stamina and verve knowing that as he keeps company with them in their suffering, they will be infused with his life-affirming power.[51]

In conclusion, this probe into Black thinkers who wrestle to find a way to engage with their heritage of oppression and come

---

50. Copeland, *Knowing Christ Crucified*, 115–16.

51. Copeland, *Knowing Christ Crucified*, 154.

out strong reveals that Black religious thought is not monolithic. By comparing the Christologies of Cone and Evans with that of Copeland, one gains something of the ferment and development in Black theology. Eddie Glaude's uncommon faith with its "hope not hopeless but unhopeful" is a sober testimony to engaging a grim reality. Yet, I want to affirm with Copeland the biblical invitation to "hope against hope" in the presence of the "God who gives life to the dead and calls into existence the things that do not exist" (Rom 4:17–18).

If our interpretation of Lamentations presents groaning as sounds in search of a witness, certainly Cone, Glaude, and Copeland exemplify features of that witness. The functional Christology of Cone presents Jesus as a witness to the double life of the freedom fighter who "percolates" involuntarily in the present system while "*voluntarily* they are preparing for its destruction." Jesus secures the heavenly home that shines its light on the upturned face of the beleaguered freedom fighter. Glaude relies on a secular cruciform model as witness that, in a sheer act of will, groaning people press on for the sake of a generation yet to come. Copeland fastens on to the witness of the resurrected Jesus who keeps company with suffering people, infusing them with his life-affirming power.

In the following chapter, the focus will be on how crucial the function of that witness is in coming alongside groaning people in the arena of ongoing hurt. It will become apparent how Black theology contributes features critical to the shape of that witness.

Chapter 7

OH, I'LL BE A WITNESS

O ur study has highlighted the crucial role of the witness to the sufferings of Lady Zion in Lamentations 1.[1] Her incessant cries to "Look! See! Compare!" make the presence of someone who pays attention absolutely critical to how she stays intact in her state of pain. If someone, especially God, could see, something might be done to help her. At least she would not be alone. By the end of Lamentations 1, no one has stepped forward, and, when someone does in Lamentations 2:13, what Zion hears is that help is nowhere to be found. The text shows that her would-be helper can affirm her situation, to be sure, but this witness has no point of reference from which to comprehend her pain and perhaps devise a plan for her relief. Her suffering is as boundless as the ocean. In the end, Lamentations' crescendo of groaning, meant to impel a witness to help, is ineffectual.[2] Though a witness has come forward, it is of little moment.

1. O'Connor, *Lamentations*, writes extensively on the role of the witness. On the search for a witness in Job, a partner who will mirror, see Brueggemann, "The Third World of Evangelical Imagination," and Brueggemann, "A Bilingual Life."

2. O'Connor, "Voices Arguing about Meaning," 28, writes: "The book is a public performance of speakers in which survivors stand up, each in turn, to tell of their particular pain and to demand God's attention. Together the voices possess only the raw harmony of common wounds, even as they offer competing and irreconcilable opinions of the disaster. God's silence leaves each voice, each testimony, standing, unrefuted, and unresolved."

In a previous chapter we argued that the canonical logic between Old and New Testaments puts forward Jesus as the groaner-in-chief whose cry from the cross encompasses the totality of the human chorus of groaning. But, like Zion in Lamentations, God is not there to hear his cry. Like Zion, Jesus has no witness. Furthermore, Holy Saturday underscores the point that no one comes forward. Jesus' burial gathers unto itself all human experience of suffering in absolute solitary confinement, in the abyss of pitch-black darkness. Easter is so astonishing because of the return of the witness to this place of total abandonment! God's raising the Son from the dead is God's way of bringing forward the only witness capable of penetrating light into the abysmal isolation of human suffering and who possesses the power to free the ones who suffer from being forever entrapped.

The resurrection powers up the gospel proclamation "The one who puts trust in Jesus will not be put to shame" (Rom 9:33; 1 Pet 2:6). Shame is a very potent destructive emotional state. In a previous study, I argued that shame as presented in Scripture refers principally to the experience of being betrayed and abandoned by one in whom you have put your trust.[3] In the case of the search for a witness to extreme loss, the gospel's claim is that God in Christ can be trusted to be the witness to that loss, epitomized in the crucifixion of the betrayed and abandoned Jesus and his resurrection. By resurrecting the crucified Jesus, God sets him beyond the reach of ultimate betrayal and abandonment. Consequently, those who cling to him receive through him the assurance of having in Jesus a constant witness to and helper in their lamentations. We will not be put to shame.

It is now time to begin to probe into what might the transformation of groaning look like as it is engaged by God who shows power to be a witness and companion to human groaning.

In Romans 8:26–27 Paul uses the phrase "sighs too deep for words" to describe how humans communicate meaning that

---

3. See Bailey, *The Self-Shaming God Who Reconciles*. This is in contrast to the view that interprets shame in the sociological context of honor-shame codes in the Mediterranean world.

exceeds the capacity of words to carry. The phrase comes out of his intimate knowledge of prayer that consists of sounds of groaning.

> Likewise the Spirit helps us in our weakness; for we do not know how to pray as we ought, but that very Spirit intercedes with sighs too deep for words. And God, who searches the heart, knows what is the mind of the Spirit, because the Spirit intercedes for the saints according to the will of God.

We must proceed with caution in assessing this text for our investigation. Whatever reference Paul might be making to glossolalia in "sighs too deep for words," the context indicates that what is being addressed here is groaning emanating out of purposeful suffering toward a goal. In context, Paul affirms in Romans 8:22–23, "We know that the whole creation has been groaning in labor pains until now; and not only the creation, but we ourselves, who have the first fruits of the Spirit, groan inwardly while we wait for adoption, the redemption of our bodies." In that remark, Paul points to the Spirit of God *both* as the fount of our complete redemption *and* as the cause of our groaning which wells up out of the acute sense of partiality awakened by the taste of the "first fruits" of the redemption of our bodies.[4] Groaning, as we have maintained, is a purposeful activity, originating out of initial experience of salvation, stretching toward fulfillment and conducted in hope. In picturing groaning in conjunction with the firstfruits of the Spirit, Paul has already set the experience within a positive trajectory culminating in a common effulgence.

However, this straining toward the goal never leaves behind the brutal realities of the moment. Beginning with v. 28, Paul asserts that our weaknesses continue to play a significant role in contributing to the partiality and deficiency out of which groaning that yearns for redemption is voiced. He contends that our weakness plumbs to depths beyond where words work. Living on the firstfruits of the Spirit while continuing to be mired in an abyss of a world in bondage to decay is an experience that eludes words

4. Parry, "Wrestling with Lamentations," 143.

adequate to articulate meaningfully in prayer. So, not only does groaning emanate from an acute sense of partiality that is awakened by the taste of "firstfruits." Groaning for redemption also encompasses sounds that emanate from life's bondage in weakness. O Lord! How long?[5]

Here begins, then, the development of a new aspect of the Spirit's response to our groanings.[6] What is new is that the context of the Spirit offers a framework of how to assess, contextualize, and transform our weaknesses. The particle "likewise" introducing Romans 8:26 projects the reader's attention forward to prepare for a frank enumeration in vv. 31–38 of the catalogue of threats that bear down upon our fragile Christian selves: criminal charges,[7] hardship, distress, persecution, famine, nakedness, peril, sword. These threats have real potential to convince us that we have been separated from the love of God, that God is not "for us," that God will not adequately prepare us. Paul cites these threats as the most likely set of circumstances to show up the partiality and deficiency of life in the Spirit that issues in groaning for redemption. Thus these circumstances are likely to be the origin of our "sighs too deep for words."

The sounds of existential threat attract a witness! Groaning is engaged by the Spirit who intercedes "with sighs too deep for words."[8] The Spirit makes our groanings the substance of the Spirit's groanings.[9] The Spirit matches the abyss of our sub-verbal-

5. The fragility of holding out amidst persistent domination is well articulated by Eddie Glaude's formulation "A hope not hopeless, but unhopeful."

6. The argument turns on taking Ὡσαύτως ("likewise") in Romans 8:26 in a comparative rather than a causal sense. See Käsemann, *Romans*, 240.

7. For Christian identity to be the cause of being prosecuted as a criminal, see Bailey, *Aliens in Your Native Land*.

8. Parry, "Prolegomena," 412, makes the brilliant canonical bridge with the sighing of the Spirit and Lamentations: "If we take the Pauline insight and connect it with our humanity-Israel-Christ-church links . . . we create the space to see the Spirit in the sufferings of Lamentations. Paul gives us a way to see the Spirit as groaning with the sufferers in Lamentations, interceding and looking for the redemption of Jerusalem."

9. Parry, "Wresting with Lamentations," 150. Smith, "The Account of Simon Magus," 743–44, points to the story of the Gerasene demoniac in Mark

ity with the depth of divine understanding and utterance.[10] The Spirit's intercession beyond words correlates with the intercession of the crucified-resurrected Christ Jesus (Rom 8:34). The burden of concern conveyed by our groaning is transformed within the family of the Trinity into what we need to remain faithful. Thus, Paul comforts his readers with the claim that God, as Father, Son, and Spirt, gathers and orders sub-verbal, confused sound, produced when we, under tremendous pressure, have gone beyond the limits of conceptualizing, and assuredly responds to our being swamped, as things are going to pieces, with that which works to our good.[11] God is for us! Nothing can separate us from the love of God in Christ Jesus.

By placing groaning within an eschatological framework of the new creation, Paul accomplishes two phases of transformation. First, he leads his readers to reimagine their groaning as a yearning forward to future fulfillment. Second, he assures them of the activity of the Spirit of God in co-speaking their expressions of despair and vulnerability and shame. This witness of the Spirit to their groaning validates them and their costly faithfulness and assures them of God's attention and support. The upshot of putting our groaning in the context of God's intention for ultimate redemption is that life is finally hopeful, and ambiguity is finally resolved, and we are strengthened to continue to fight for liberation.[12]

5:1–13 as a mirror image: "When believers do not know what to say in prayer, the Spirit dwelling in them, using their voices, makes supplication on their behalf with inarticulate groanings. This is the same belief which we meet in the Gospels where Jesus questions the demons dwelling in a man and they answer him, using the man's voice."

10. Wolff, *Anthropology*, 60, points to the conjectured reading of Proverbs 20:27, "Yahweh watches over the breath of man/he searches all the innermost parts of the body."

11. I am keenly aware that in our post-Holocaust world statements about God working all things to our good are deeply problematic. As the virus rages on, this statement will be repudiated by many. It is only by the singular stroke of the resurrection of Jesus Christ from his evil and unjustified crucifixion and the utter trust in the gospel that he is the One in whom all things are raised to new life that Paul's statement can be proffered.

12. This insistence on liberation is a major contribution of the thinking of

Oh, I'll Be a Witness

The emergence of a witness is a key indicator that transformation of groaning is possible. The Trinitarian exposition of the cross and resurrection stakes out the framework of this contextualization and transformation by presenting Jesus as the chief witness to our pain. This exposition presents the claim that the Father's abandonment of the Son on the cross and the utter forsakenness of the Son on Holy Saturday is meant to shape such a witness who is stood up in the eruption of the joy of the resurrection. This claim is fundamental to a Christian possibility of the transformation of groaning.[13]

Within the family of God as Trinity, the Spirit is a co-speaker with those who groan with "sighs too deep for words." Our groans become part of the vast expanse of the Spirit's groans. This intercession maps onto the intercession before the Father of the resurrected Christ who continues to bear the wounds of his crucifixion to show solidarity with those driven to abandonment. The evangelistic call invites groaners to act in trust and to place our plight within the vast breadth of the Trinity's embrace of pain. Our trust is made secure in the resurrection's demonstration of God's ultimate triumph over suffering and God's ushering in of an immeasurably different new creation.

Our entrustment of pain within the Trinity, so conceived, sets up the possibility of a conviction growing within the believer that no trauma is powerful enough to separate the groaner from the love of God. This conviction offers "protection for the self against terror by remembering terror"[14] within the family of God. When those who are driven to groaning contextualize their burden of concern within this framework, a change is ripe to occur in their emotive state that registers publicly. This change can take myriad forms, and our discussion below will only touch on a few.

James Cone.

13. I recognize the existence of other religious traditions which offer their distinctive frameworks for transformation.

14. This suggestive phrase is offered by Dyson, *Holler If You Hear Me*, 227–28, cited in Perkinson, "Illin' the Evil," 374.

A less analytical way to recast our position is to inquire what might happen when the tears of the world are read through the tears of the Trinity.[15] The African American spiritual "Nobody knows the trouble I've seen; nobody knows but Jesus" points to him as chief witness. Those who give themselves to this claim receive a critical assist to their flagging dignity by way of the inner assurance that they are not alone, that they are important enough to draw down a witness, a companion, that they are not left to a grim fate, that together "a way can be made out of no way."[16] Shelly Rambo adds perceptively, "If the cross is the symbol that denies value to some lives then the return of Jesus, the defiled one, reassigns value to those denied value."[17]

Outwardly, this change in perspective may be indicated by the surprising eruption of praise and a desire to tell out the greatness of the God in their lives, to be themselves a witness to their being given a witness.[18] As we have demonstrated already, worship is a time and space that is laden with potential for this transformation to be experienced and shared. Hymns and spiritual songs alike bring to voice the testimony of transformation. For example, both the gospel song "Precious Lord, take my hand, lead me on, help me stand . . . lead me home,"[19] and the hymn, "Sometimes a light surprises the child of God who sings," testify to the conviction that even though the singer is trapped in nothingness, "yet God the same abiding, his praise shall tune my voice; for while in him confiding, I cannot but rejoice."[20]

---

15. A phrase suggested by Parry, "Prolegomena," 410, and O'Conner, *Lamentations*.

16. This was the theme of an exhibit at the National Museum of African American History, Washington, DC.

17. Rambo, *Resurrecting Wounds*, 102.

18. For a demonstration of this transformation in Psalm 73, see Bailey, *The Self-Shaming God*, 19–24.

19. "Precious Lord, Take My Hand," in *Glory to God: The Presbyterian Hymnal*, 834.

20. "Sometimes a Light Surprises," in *Glory to God: The Presbyterian Hymnal*, 800.

Additionally, when the traumatized integrate the idea that their tears may be comprehended through the tears of God, a new pathway leading to restored dignity, even in their degradation, opens up. This dignity gives them cause to mount a protest against their oppressors and oppressive conditions and insist on change. Moreover, the record of their lamentations becomes the template for future generations of readers to view their current situation and make similar protests for change.[21]

Conversely, we must also ask what the implications for those in power when the tears of the Trinity are read through the tears of the world. What might our response be to the realization that human groaning causes God to cry? For example, when Lamentations is read as a record of oppressors' infliction of brutal suffering on a supine people, we have shown that canonical logic opens that record of suffering to be a proximate cause of the pain of the suffering servant, the man of sorrows and acquainted with grief. When the metaphor of the servant is adopted toward understanding the person and work of Jesus, then oppressors are put on notice that their outrageously inhumane atrocities take an unplanned trajectory toward a target that should unnerve and unseat them. *Jesus cries* because of what we have done or are doing. The *Spirit's sighs* are wailed with human sounds too deep for words. Parry comments perceptively, "In this dangerous, almost prophetic, mode the word of God comes as a harsh word of rebuke, a shocking exposure of an oft-forgotten crime, a call to the painful task of listening to one's victims."[22]

The weight of this intervention upon the perpetrator is pregnant of causing significant changes. First, the pressure may start a process of awakening to the long stretch of prejudices and biases that have formed us, both individually and collectively. For example, racism lives within us for a long time. It becomes part of how

---

21. See Yansen, *Daughter Zion's Trauma*, 24, 32.

22. Parry, "Wrestling with Lamentations," 131. See also Parry, "Lamentations and Politics of Prayer," 84. "It is always a temptation for the politically powerful to avoid looking at those adversely affected by their decisions. Lamentations calls to its users to look very hard indeed."

we understand ourselves and renders the suffering we cause invisible to ourselves.[23] Becoming aware of one's involvement in the tears of God, because one is caught in a system where one benefits from the ongoing trauma of the vulnerable, can be a profoundly wounding experience of humility and shame. However, it can be a moment of possibility. The possibility of significant change begins with confession. Here remembering the insight of James Baldwin brought forward by Eddie Glaude is pivotal: "They have never confessed their crimes, and they don't know how to confess their crimes. . . . If you can't confess, you can't be forgiven, and if you can't be forgiven, you can't get past it. . . . The only way to get past it is to confess."[24]

One must do the hard work through the dynamics of denial, fear, and the insidious operations of privilege. This means that this work is done in the register of the affections, in which groaning may play a part. Out of that hurtful experience of having one's eyes opened, a new possibility opens up to see oneself held by the One who bore our transgressions and was bruised for our iniquities. Being held by that One who also holds the groans of racism's victims, a person can emerge within a new company of grief[25] as a witness to the suffering brought on by white supremacy, joining the voices of the suffering ones in the fight to claim life under new terms.

Second, it is helpful to remember Robert's axiom that an emotion is a "concerned-based construal."[26] When victims of oppression display a deep and searching acceptance of the oppressors' admission of responsibility for their suffering and when such victims offer an equally heartfelt forgiveness and reconciliation to the oppressors, this can generate among oppressors an emotional overflow of gratitude, a will to make reparation, and advocacy for change. A polity that is shaped by these kinds of emotional states widens the circle of power in order to make political policy that

23. See Rambo, *Resurrecting Wounds*, 73–79.
24. Cited in Glaude, "The Country That Refused to Change," 85.
25. This suggestive phrase comes from Glaude, "The Pandemic Will Pass."
26. See the chapter "Making Sense of Groaning."

supports the flourishing of life. Seeing the tears of God in the tears of the world can be a motivator for action, both against injustice and for love, as the Spirit gathers up the people of God into responsive and creative action.[27]

The Role of Lamentations in the Care of Moral Injury after War

Our study of the place of the witness comes to a conclusion by turning to a relatively new front of usefulness for Lamentations: the care of those who suffer moral injury after war. This topic is not unrelated to the foregoing discussion, which has been framed broadly along the lines of systemic racism. The relationship between moral injury and racism is that in both cases groaning attends the experience of shattered structures of meaning that once supported those who dominate, and the contextualization of that groaning is critical to a rebuilding of a new structure. We begin with a reminder of the historical situation that gave rise to Lamentations.

The book of Lamentations is most likely a literary commentary from a circle of adherents to Israel's God who are suffering the effects of being conquered by overwhelming military forces of Babylonia. Israel's literature of the postexilic era indicates that while "Assyria's violence against North Israel was bad enough . . . Babylon, because of their concerns to keep Egypt from controlling the Levant, inflicted even more violence, utterly destroying cities in order to keep the Egyptians from benefitting from the cities of the Levant."[28] Through the poetry of Lamentations, Israel constructed a narrative created out of collective trauma under the blunt force of Babylon's might.

The writers of Lamentations created poetry to describe the pain the survivors carried with them. It is based, to be sure, in the realities of siege warfare, military alliances, and land battles,

27. Parry, "Wrestling with Lamentations," 144.

28. Foster, *The Theology of the Books of Haggai and Zechariah*, 65, who cites Stager, "The Fury of Babylon," 56–69, 76–77.

but the poetry is so skillfully written that it is able to be accessed on deep emotional and relational levels by readers who are far removed from the sixth century BCE. The recent interest in reading Lamentations from the perspective of current trauma studies is evidence of the book's openness, its quality of being an unfinished work. Our discussions of Lamentations 1 and, to a lesser extent, Lamentations 2 have been enhanced by this trauma-based reading which has yielded new insights into the rationale of the sometimes-chaotic flow of the poetry and of the roles played by its cast of speakers.

A special area of trauma care is the spiritual care of persons who have suffered moral injury as the result of military action, including both service personnel and civilians.[29] Pastoral care specialists who study moral injury, joining with biblical scholars, have noticed the potential Lamentations holds for supplying lyrical structure and metaphorical imagery that resonates with morally injured combatants and civilians. The profound spiritual crises into which persons so injured are plunged are plain to see in the ancient text and can be grasped by the injured.

The text itself functions as a witness to such suffering. As such, it retains unto itself the potential of contributing to the transformation of one who is calling out for someone to see and stand with them. We will conclude this chapter by exploring how Lamentations can foster bearing witness as a form of "witness poetry," that is, poetry that recognizes "the tragic, traumatic, and violent experiences of war-related losses and to sustain lamentation for these losses with the expectation of finding ways to live with moral injury."[30]

Nancy Ramsay defines military moral injury as "a recent term that describes the ancient insight that, in addition to physical wounds, war wounds the souls of those who, in combat, transgress otherwise deeply held values related to human life because they

29. For more information on this type of specialized pastoral care, contact the Soul Repair Center for Moral Injury after War at Brite Divinity School, Texas Christian University, Fort Worth, Texas.

30. Fawson, "Sustaining Lamentation," 43.

kill and maim one another and often innocent civilians."[31] Fawson adds that military moral injury is "not merely a state of cognitive dissonance, but a *state of loss of trust* in previously deeply held beliefs about one's own or others' ability to keep our shared moral covenant."[32] Indicators of moral injury include "grief, shame and guilt, anger, loss of meaning and purpose, imaginations burdened by facing a level of radical evil they could not previously have imagined and cradling only tenuous hope."[33]

Another feature of moral injury is ambiguous loss. Ramsay develops helpfully this concept by locating it within the "ambiguities that insinuate historical life and revise any illusion of mastery or control."[34] Ambiguous loss shatters a soldier's "ability to imagine themselves as good persons acting in a world ordered by a divine agency that limits destructive evil."[35] Lamentations likewise wells up out of the demonstration that Israel's worldview of being under the protection of a divine agency is in tatters.

Ambiguous loss resonates with the tensions within Israel's statecraft in the sixth century BCE. Israel followed the customary strategies of making foreign alliances, not anticipating being betrayed by allies in fear of Babylon's might. Ambiguous loss can be seen in the oscillation in Lamentations 1 between confession of sin (naming realistically what one can be accountable for) and the overkill of suffering, or the oscillation between the prudential alliances made with foreign nations and the judgments of prophets that this runs afoul of total loyalty to Yahweh. This is the ambiguity that colors the trauma of the collapse of the state.

However, moral injury is not sustained only on the battlefield. Ramsay makes the point that "tragically, for some combatants, moral injury arises when they experience religious and racial prejudice from supposed comrades or when they experience no justice after military sexual trauma perpetrated by comrades on

31. Ramsay, "Moral Injury," 142.

32. Fawson, "Sustaining Lamentation," 43.

33. Ramsay, "Moral Injury," 143.

34. Ramsay, "Moral Injury as Loss and Grief," 144.

35. Ramsay, "Moral Injury as Loss and Grief," 160.

whom they must rely in battle."[36] The suffering of military members deepens when they "are shamed by power-laden, socially constructed, and sustained experiences of oppression and privilege such as racism, sexism and Christianism."[37]

Those who reach out to care for the morally wounded often encounter soldiers in similar states of isolation because no one could possibly understand what they are experiencing. Frequently, their suffering is exacerbated by the sense that God is unreachable, indifferent, and hostile. As we have illustrated, these are aspects of the anti-shepherd of Lamentations, and the frank portrayal of this symbol has the power to connect with the shattered faith of the morally injured. To be reminded of Elizabeth Boase's observation: "Within Lamentations, divine absence and violent presence stand in contrast with each other, a contrast which creates tension in the text. . . . The presence of the Babylonians as the actual enemy is sidelined, with Yahweh portrayed as the enemy. Violent presence is a past experience of the divine, while the sense of divine absence is a present reality. The ongoing pain comes from divine absence in the wake of the active destruction."[38] At its most basic level, Lamentations connects with those who feel mired in the abyss.

Ramsay brings to our attention that even though Lamentations' imagery is ancient and culture-bound, militarily morally injured persons can see themselves reflected in its verses. The laments of Lamentations resonate with the shame, guilt, betrayal, and anger that haunt survivors of military moral injury and impede their recovery following conflict. Taking up what Ramsay has noticed we can expand her insight in light of our analysis of Lamentations to show how the book yields a rich trove of possibilities that relate to the care of the morally injured by war.

Lamentations 1 is full of imagery taken from combat. Elucidation of the list of examples that follows may be found in our earlier discussion in chapter 3: betrayal by political leaders and trusted allies (vv. 2, 17, 19), the crumpling of military forces before

36. Ramsay, "Moral Injury as Loss and Grief," 143.

37. Ramsay, "Moral Injury as Loss and Grief," 144.

38. Boase, "Constructing Meaning," 466.

a superior force (vv .6, 15), being shamed and demeaned in one's body (v. 8), experiencing the powerlessness of divine protection (v. 10), the privations of siege warfare (v. 11 and especially 2:11–12; 4:10 leading to cannibalism), battle tactics that overwhelm (vv. 13–14), urban warfare (v. 20), desire for revenge (vv. 21–22).

Paramount, however, is the constant cry of groaning, which is meant both to convey deeply felt emotion that is simply beyond the capacity of words to convey and which is meant to attract a witness. Equally as pregnant with possibility for resonance is the silence of God as witness or the absence of any human witness who could understand enough to possibly help. The role of the witness in Lamentations is crucial and the search for an effective one is desperate. The book is a witness to those who realize that there is no witness adequate to the task of comprehending and relieving.

The special quality of Lamentations as witness poetry is not confined to its potential to connect with and bring out latent memories, feelings, and questions, however. Recall that the book ends with an "if" clause stating an assessment, followed by a "then," which introduces a blank conclusion: "If you have utterly rejected us, and are angry with us beyond measure, then . . . ." The open-endedness of the book presents the opportunity to explore a range of options to "fill in the blank."

As we have seen, Second Isaiah presents a source that supplies a radical option. God's clarion call for comfort reverses the abysmal fear that ends Lamentations. The striking portrayal of the suffering servant, which we have explored earlier, could open itself up to being grasped by someone who is overcome by grief, shame, and guilt. This figure had no power to control the suffering placed upon him and did not shrink from being seen as shot through with grief, shame, and guilt. God made the servant for a specific mission, to be a point of solidarity with everyone who is in like manner burdened and through that solidarity to be the center of a healing community.[39] If a witness is someone who genuinely

39. Again, I call attention to the strong repudiation of Isaiah 53:10, "it was the will of the Lord to bruise him," to the assertion of Lamentations 3:33, "for [the Lord] does not willingly afflict or grieve anyone." The negation of this claim is also strongly supported by the ending of Lamentations. Interpreters

empathizes and understands, surely God made the servant have the life experiences he had precisely in order to fulfill that role, and thus to join with the veteran in the journey toward healing by bringing a suffering one out of isolation into community and out of shame into the honoring of his or her situation.

The most radical of witnesses, of course, is the cruciform model of Jesus that we have been depicting in this book. What transpired in the crucifixion and burial of Jesus represents the worst of all conclusions, the sum of all human fears, doubts, isolation, and anguish. In the fulfillment of his mission, Jesus suffers the trauma of being abandoned by the God who sent him on his mission and in whom he trusted. He is made to suffer being blotted out by the enmity of an empire. In his death and burial he exemplifies the logical conclusion that the ending of Lamentations requires.

Yet, astonishingly, he is resurrected, brought back from the abyss of nonentity, as the type of the new human God sets out as the promise and claim for all. This new human both carries the scars of the past but nevertheless is possessed of a new lease on living with integrity. As the new human, Jesus is a double witness. He can reach out to those who are afflicted by trauma because they see themselves mirrored sensitively in him. In the camaraderie, the walking together of like with like, he is the witness to the new future that awaits his wounded comrades. In his witness to their shared future he creates openings for healing to begin. So God gives the evidence of a divinely fierce tenderness that undergirds the traumatized through their entire lives.[40]

---

must keep in mind that Lamentations is the product of a community's wrestling with the destruction of their state and thus contains many voices in that conversation.

40. Ramsay's essay is noteworthy for bringing an intersectional perspective to moral injury, highlighting in particular when that injury is the result of racial prejudice. Our earlier investigation of Black religion in chapters 5 and 6 suggested three representative responses to groaning—Jesus as a pattern for survival (Cone), a hope, not hopeless, but unhopeful (Glaude), and the eschatological power of a vulnerable Christ (Copeland). Of the three, the latter one is the most congruent with the model of care outlined here.

In one of the resurrection appearances of Jesus, a mangled man materializes amongst his shell-shocked and spirit-shattered friends and shows them his wounds. He invites us to place ourselves with our wounds inside his wounds and to walk with him, wounded comrade with wounded comrade, into a future that offers dignity and community.[41] The imagery has roots in Jesus' encounter with Thomas in John 20:24–29,[42] but that is not the only place where the picture occurs in Christian Scripture of the wounded walking into new life. The figure of Isaac offers consideration of someone who will always carry with him the eternally wounding memory of seeing his father looming over him with a raised knife, yet his name offers him a way to live up to its meaning, "laughter." The figure of Jacob, limping for the rest of his life but benefitting from securing a blessing from an assailant after an all-night fight, is another signature model. The Ethiopian eunuch continues on his way "rejoicing" after being baptized.[43] The story of the meeting of Mary and Jesus on Easter morning discussed earlier provides yet another image.

These models portray a stature of resilience. Resilience is a solid transformational result of the cruciform model. Resilience responds to an acknowledgment that life can never be restored to its previous condition, yet without succumbing to despair.[44] Ramsay insists that it is crucial to recognize that ambiguous loss implies ambiguous control. We have limited ability to control what happens. Some causes for loss are beyond our control. Resilience emerges when we go to the larger frame of meaning of the resurrected crucified Jesus and lodge within that symbol our admission

---

41. See Edward Schillito's poem "Jesus of the Scars":
  The other gods were strong; but Thou wast weak;
  They rode, but Thou didst stumble to a throne;
  But to our wounds only God's wounds can speak,
  And not a god has wounds, but Thou alone.

42. See the probing interpretation by Rambo, *Resurrecting Wounds*, of the Thomas story as it is interpreted through the painting by Caravaggio (ca. 1601–2).

43. I am grateful to Jeremy Williams for calling this to my attention.

44. Rambo, *Resurrecting Wounds*, 5.

of our limits of control and do our mourning of memories and surface our haunting behaviors.[45] We will always carry what we admit in sorrow, but we trust a God who has shown in the resurrected wounded Jesus that, despite the wounds we carry, we can have in him a future that is good and honorable.[46] For those who struggle for racial justice, here is another possibility for a model for their arduous work.

In the presence of the crucified and resurrected Christ, one finds a safe space to voice the unspeakable. Nancy Ramsay adds, "This is the space safe enough to voice and explore whether there is a credible meaning or belief system that can sustain the veteran going forward."[47] The Spirit with sighs too deep for words is the co-speaker of our questions: Is hope an available option? Is forgiveness available?[48]

The church is a place where the journey toward resiliency might begin. The community of God's people are called to be this safe space where the traumatized can find sanctuary. A sanctuary has space for hospitality and conversation.[49] Here the witness to and with the veteran is crucial. When the morally injured service veteran comes to the safe place, he or she has likely suffered the loss of trust in once deeply held values. Caregivers frequently comment on this loss of trust as "a loss of soul." This actually may begin in the onset of training, only to be exacerbated in combat. Returning from war, the veteran may be without soul: isolated, full of shame, anger, and fear. Care of soul is the return of "soul" to the

---

45. Ramsay, "Moral Injury as Loss and Grief," 164.

46. Rambo, *Resurrecting Wounds*, 6–7, 11. This construal of the way forward is similar to the formulation of Eddie Glaude: "At the moment of the transformation a world, a different way of being in the world, is made possible, and it is within this space of brokenness we make ourselves and the world anew" (*Uncommon Faith*, 53–54).

47. Ramsay, "Moral Injury as Loss and Grief," 163.

48. Ramsay, "Moral Injury as Loss and Grief," 164.

49. The growing awareness of the church's ministry to injured service personnel is seen in a complete issue of the *Presbyterian Outlook* organized around helping congregations to a better understanding of and care for Military Moral Injury. See especially in that issue Ott, "Killing," 26–31.

veteran in such a way that he or she can begin to imagine a future based on trust, even while living in the ongoingness of the wounds of war. Indispensable to the return of soul is work with a circle of witnesses who will uphold the veteran's story of harm done and harm suffered and who will share with the veteran their own hurt. In the circle of witnesses, "my hurt knows your hurt, and it goes to it."[50] Within the conversation, the Spirit is a co-speaker of pain and fear. Rambo adds helpfully, "It is not just that one's 'hurt' recognizes the hurt in another, but that the collective attunement to pain forges routes of healing that did not previously exist."[51]

The cry of Lamentations to "Look! See!" is the cry of the soul damaged veteran. The journey that begins in the safe place is "a journey initiated by the work of the eyes."[52] Rambo elaborates, "By looking someone in the eye, you are not just looking *at* them, you are looking *into* them, as if to clear the way for deeper truths to emerge. . . . And once you have that instant attachment, then you see it growing and you could see openness—relaxation, more openness, more actual feelings rather than stories. . . . They started talking about how they felt and that's when the real growth took place."[53] There is a critical tie between the return of soul and the community that looks and sees, that holds the hurt. The soul does not belong to you alone.

The safe space of the church also supports the enactment of the journey toward resilience through the power of ritual. Ramsay summarizes the possibility of ritual, which I affirm:

> Ritual practices are useful in spiritual care with veterans because ritual offers individual and communal opportunities for reasserting our personal and communal trust in a social and cosmic order that is stronger than the horizon of destructive violence war discloses. Rituals augment practices of care by helping veterans recover their trust in the mythic dimensions of their faith experience.

50. Rambo, *Resurrecting Wounds*, 126.
51. Rambo, *Resurrecting Wounds*, 130.
52. Rambo, *Resurrecting Wounds*, 134.
53. Rambo, *Resurrecting Wounds*, 120.

> Ritual action is performative. Engaging in ritual prac-
> tice asserts that ritual realty as available and true, both
> personally and communally. This performative power of
> ritual practice assists those isolated by shame and guilt to
> recover access to communal and relational ties.[54]

Rituals of reconciliation that include the use of water in a remembrance of one's baptism hold the possibility of confessing one's accountability while simultaneously rooting one's spirit in the cleansing love of God. The Eucharist with its tactile ritual elements of bread and wine enfolds the worshiper in Christ's broken body and shed blood. The ministry of music may sweep one powerfully up into new feelings of freedom. We have already noticed this in the way Black churches reach for spirituals and gospel songs to express trauma and enact freedom. The ancient service of Evensong might provide a similar setting for reflection and sustenance. Preaching, as we have noticed in exploring worship in the Black church, is a performative ritual where the speaker enacts the freedom being proclaimed.

Another option to explore is to imitate the poet of Lamentations 1 and turn a psalm of confidence inside-out to create a medium for expressing the lostness of moral injury. Options might include Psalms 130, 131, or 133. These might be shared in a circle of witnesses for added reflection. This might be followed by texts that engage feelings of abandonment and deprecation, such as Isaiah 40:27–31 or Psalm 42–43. The witness of a text that can be accessed repeatedly and wrestled with on various levels may contribute to regaining resiliency.

"You are my witnesses." The Gospel of Matthew includes these words as some of the very last words the resurrected-crucified Jesus spoke to his disciples before he was taken way from earthly life with them. In his name we can dare to answer the cry of Lady Zion and all her children thenceforward, "Look and see if there be any sorrow like my sorrow." In his name we can dare to sing, "Oh! I'll be a witness for my Lord." I will join my voice with yours.

54. Ramsay, "Moral Injury as Loss and Grief," 162.

Bibliography

Alexander, Jeffrey, et al. *Cultural Trauma and Collective Identity.* Berkeley: University of California Press, 2004.

Allen, Leslie C. *A Liturgy for Grief: A Pastoral Commentary on Lamentations.* Grand Rapids: Baker Academics, 2011.

Attridge, Harold W. "'Heard Because of His Reverence,' (Heb 5:7)." *Journal of Biblical Literature* 98.1 (1979) 90–93.

Bailey, Warner M. *Aliens in Your Native Land, 1 Peter and the Formation of Christian Identity.* Eugene, OR: Pickwick, 2020.

———. *Living in the Language of God: Wise Speaking in the Book of the Twelve.* Eugene, OR: Pickwick, 2017.

———. *The Self-Shaming God Who Reconciles: A Pastoral Response to Abandonment within the Christian Canon.* Eugene, OR: Pickwick, 2013.

Bailey, Wilma Ann. "The Lament Traditions of Enslaved African American Women and the Lament Traditions of the Hebrew Bible." In *Lamentations in Ancient and Contemporary Cultural Contexts,* edited by Nancy C. Lee and Carleen Mandolfo, 139–50. Atlanta: Society of Biblical Literature, 2008.

Bakhtin, Mikhail. *Problems in Dostoevsky's Poetics.* Edited by G. Emerson; Theory and History of Literature 8. Minneapolis: University of Minnesota Press, 1984.

———. *Speech Genres and Other Late Essays.* Translated by Vern W. McGee, edited by Caryl Emerson and Michael Holquist. Austin: University of Texas Press, 1986.

Baldwin, James. *The Fire Next Time.* New York: Dell, 1946.

Baldwin, Lewis V. "'Deliverance to the Captives': Images of Jesus Christ in the Minds of Afro-American Slaves." *Journal of Religious Studies* 12.2 (1986) 27–45.

Bauckham, Richard. "God's Self-Identification with the Godforsaken in the Gospel of Mark." In *Jesus and the God of Israel: God Crucified and Other Studies on the New Testament's Christology of Divine Identity,* 254–68. Milton Keynes, UK: Paternoster, 2008.

Boase, Elizabeth. "Constructing Meaning in the Face of Suffering: Theodicy in Lamentations." *Vetus Testamentum* 58 (2009) 449–68.

———. "The Traumatized Body." In *Trauma and Traumatization in Individual and Collective Dimensions, Insights from Biblical Studies and Beyond*, edited by Eve-Marie Becker et al., 193–209. Studia Aarhusiana Neotestamentica 2. Göttingen: Vandenhoeck & Ruprecht, 2014.

Bonhoeffer, Dietrich. *"After Ten Years."* Introduction by Victoria J. Barnett. Minneapolis: Fortress, 2017.

Brooks, David. "Mental Health in the Age of the Coronavirus." *New York Times*, April 2, 2020.

Brown, Sterling. "Negro Folk Expression: Spirituals, Seculars, Ballads and Work Songs." In *The Making of Black America: The Black Community in Modern America*, edited by August Meier and Elliott Rudwick, 2:209–26. New York: Atheneum, 1974.

Brueggemann, Walter. "A Bilingual Life." In *The Threat of Life, Sermons on Pain, Power, and Weakness*, 83–89. Minneapolis: Fortress, 1996.

———. *Old Testament Theology: An Introduction.* Nashville: Abingdon, 2008.

———. "The Rhetoric of Hurt and Hope, Ethics Odd and Crucial." *Annual of the Society of Christian Ethics* (1989) 73–92.

———. "A Shattered Transcendence: Exile and Restoration." In *Biblical Theology, Problems and Perspectives: Essays in Honor of J. Christiaan Beker*, edited by Steven J. Kraftchick et al., 169–82. Nashville: Abingdon, 1995.

———. "The Third World of Evangelical Imagination." In *Interpretation and Obedience: From Faithful Reading to Faithful Living*, 9–27. Minneapolis: Fortress, 1991.

Buchanan, George. *To the Hebrews.* Anchor Bible 36. Garden City, NY: Doubleday, 1972.

Buthelezi, Manas. "The Theological Meaning of True Humanity." In *The Challenge of Black Theology in South Africa*, edited by Basil Moore, 93–103. Atlanta: John Knox, 1974.

Cavell, Stanley. "Hope Against Hope." In *Emerson's Transcendental Ethics*, edited by David Justin Hodge, 171–82. Stanford: Stanford University Press, 2003.

Childs, Brevard S. "Retrospective Reading of the Old Testament Prophets." *Zeitschrift für die alttestamentliche Wissenschaft* 108 (1996) 362–77.

Cleage, Albert. *The Black Messiah.* New York: Sheed and Ward, 1968.

Collins, Terence. "The Physiology of Tears in the Old Testament: Part I." *Catholic Biblical Quarterly* 33 (1971) 18–38.

Cone, James H. *A Black Theology of Liberation: Twentieth Anniversary Edition.* Maryknoll, NY: Orbis, 1990.

———. *The Cross and the Lynching Tree.* Maryknoll, NY: Orbis, 2011.

———. *God of the Oppressed.* New York: Seabury, 1975.

———. *The Spirituals and the Blues: An Interpretation.* Maryknoll, NY: Orbis, 1992.

Copeland, M. Shawn. *Knowing Christ Crucified: The Witness of African American Religious Experience.* Maryknoll, NY: Orbis, 2018.

Dietrich, Jan. "Cultural Traumata in the Ancient Near East." In *Trauma and Traumatization in Individual and Collective Dimensions: Insights from Biblical Studies and Beyond*, edited by Eve-Marie Becker et al., 145–61. Studia Aarhusiana Neotestamentica 2. Göttingen: Vandenhoeck & Ruprecht, 2014.

Du Bois, W. E. B. *The Souls of Black Folk*. In *W. E. B. Du Bois: Writings*, edited by Nathan Huggins, 357–548. New York: Library of America, 1995.

Dyson, Michael Eric. *Holler If You Hear Me: Searching for Tupac Shakur*. New York: Basic, 2001.

Evans, James H., Jr. *We Have Been Believers: An African American Systematic Theology*. Minneapolis: Fortress, 2015.

Fawson, Shawn "Sustaining Lamentation for Military Moral Injury: Witness Poetry That Bears the Traces of Extremity." In *Military Moral Injury and Spiritual Care: A Resource for Religious Leaders and Professional Caregivers*, edited by Nancy J. Ramsay and Carrie Doehring, 42–54. St. Louis: Chalice, 2019.

Foster, Robert L. *The Theology of the Books of Haggai and Zechariah*. Cambridge: Cambridge University Press, 2021.

Freedman, Samuel G. "Laying Claim to Sorrow Beyond Words." *New York Times*, December 13, 1997, section B7.

Gibbs, Nancy. "The Only Way Forward." *Time*, November 12, 2018, 23.

Gladney, Larry. "A Devastating and Ruinous History." *Yale Alumni Magazine*, July-August, 2020, 37–38.

Glaude, Eddie S., Jr. "Anger and the 'Accumulated Grievance' of Black America." NPR interview, May 29, 2020. www.pbs.org/video/glaude-1590786006.

———. "The Country That Refused to Change." *Time*, July 6, 2020.

———. *Democracy in Black: How Race Still Enslaves the American Soul*. New York: Crown, 2016.

———. "George Floyd's Murder Shows Once More That We Cannot Wait for White America to End Racism." *Time*, May 29, 2020.

———. "The Magician's Serpent: Race and the Tragedy of American Democracy." *James Baldwin Review* 5 (2019) 9–22.

———. "The Pandemic Will Pass: Our Grief Will Endure." *Washington Post*, April 6, 2020.

———. "Princeton Prof. on Race Relations: 'Our Democracy Is Broken.'" PBS interview, September 15, 2020. https://www.pbs.org/wnet/amanpour-and-company/video/princeton-prof-on-race-relations-our-democracy-is-broken/.

———. "Racism We've Seen in Trump Era Is Not New. It's Just Louder." WDET Radio Interview, November 20, 2020. https://wdet.org/posts/2020/11/20/90321-eddie-glaude-racism-weve-seen-in-trump-era-is-not-new-its-just-louder/.

———. *An Uncommon Faith, A Pragmatic Approach to the Study of African American Religion*. Athens: University of Georgia Press, 2018.

————. "We Cannot Wait for White America to End Racism." *Time*, June 15, 2020.

Glory to God: The Presbyterian Hymnal. Louisville, KY: Westminster John Knox, 2013.

Hillers, Delbert R. *Lamentations: Introduction, Translation, and Notes.* Anchor Bible 7A. Garden City, NY: Doubleday, 1973.

Holt, Else K. "Daughter Zion: Trauma, Cultural Memory and Gender in Old Testament Poetics." In *Trauma and Traumatization in Individual and Collective Dimensions: Insights from Biblical Studies and Beyond*, edited by Eve-Marie Becker et al., 162–76. Studia Aarhusiana Neotestamentica 2. Göttingen: Vandenhoeck & Ruprecht, 2014.

Hurston, Nora Neal. *Mules and Men.* New York: Harper Perennial Library, 1970.

Jaspers, Karl. *The Origin and Goal of History.* New Haven, CT: Yale University Press, 1953.

Käsemann, Ernst. *Commentary on Romans.* Translated and edited by Geoffrey W. Bromiley. Grand Rapids: Eerdmans, 1980.

————. "The Pauline Theology of the Cross." *Interpretation* 24 (1970) 151–77.

————. "The Saving Significance of the Death of Jesus in Paul." In *Perspectives on Paul*, 32–59. Philadelphia: Fortress, 1969.

Kierkegaard, Søren. "The Sickness unto Death." In *A Kierkegaard Anthology*, edited by Robert Bretall, 339–91. New York: Modern Library, 1946.

Landy, Francis. "Lamentations". In *The Literary Guide to the Bible*, edited by Robert Alter and Frank Kermode, 329–34. Cambridge: Harvard University Press, 1987.

Levine, Daniel. *Healing the Reason-Emotion Split: Scarecrows, Tin Woodmen, and the Wizard.* London: Routledge, 2021.

Lewis, Alan E. *Between Cross and Resurrection: A Theology of Holy Saturday.* Grand Rapids: Eerdmans, 2001.

Lewis, C. S. *A Grief Observed.* Greenwich, CN: Seabury, 1961.

Linafelt, Tod. "The Refusal of a Conclusion in the Book of Lamentations." *Journal of Biblical Literature* 120 (2001) 340–43.

————. *Surviving Lamentations, Catastrophize, Lament, and Protest in the Afterlife of a Biblical Book.* Chicago: University of Chicago Press, 2000.

————. "Surviving Lamentations (One More Time)." In *Lamentations in Ancient and Contemporary Cultural Context*, edited by Nancy C. Lee and Carleen Mandolfo, 57–66. Symposium Series 43. Atlanta: Society of Biblical Literature, 2008.

Maier, Christi M. "Body Space as Public Space: Jerusalem's Wounded Body in Lamentations." In *Construction of Space II: The Biblical City and Other Imagined Spaces*, edited by Jon L. Berquist and Claudia V. Camp, 119–38. London: T. & T. Clark, 2008.

Mandolfo, Carleen. "Dialogic Form Criticism: An Intertextual Reading of Lamentations and Psalms of Lament." In *Bakhtin and Genre Theory in Biblical Studies*, edited by Roland T. Boer, 69–90. Atlanta: Society of Biblical Literature, 2007.

Mays, Benjamin E. *The Negro's God: As Reflected in His Literature*. Preface by Vincent Harding. 1938. Reprint, New York: Athenium, 1969.

Miller, Charles William. "Reading Voices: Personification, Dialogism, and the Reader of Lamentations 1." *Biblical Interpretation* 9 (2001) 393–408.

Miller, Patrick D. "Heaven's Prisoners: The Lament in Christian Prayer." In *Lament: Reclaiming Practices in Pulpit, Pew, and Public Square*, edited by Nancy A Brown and Patrick D. Miller, 15–26. Louisville, KY: Westminster John Knox, 2005.

———. *Interpreting the Psalms*. Philadelphia: Westminster, 1986.

O'Connor, Kathleen M. "How Trauma Studies Can Contribute to Old Testament Studies." In *Trauma and Traumatization in Individual and Collective Dimensions: Insights from Biblical Studies and Beyond*, edited by Eve-Marie Becker et al., 210–22. Studia Aarhusiana Neotestamentica 2. Göttingen: Vandenhoeck & Ruprecht, 2014.

———. *Lamentations and The Tears of the World*. Maryknoll, NY: Orbis, 2002.

———. "Voices Arguing about Meaning." In *Lamentations in Ancient and Contemporary Cultural Contexts*, edited by Nancy C. Lee and Carleen Mandolfo, 27–32. Atlanta: Society of Biblical Literature, 2008.

Ott, Daniel J. "Killing." *Presbyterian Outlook*, October 25, 2021, 26–31.

Outka, Paul. "Whitman and Race ('He's Queer, He's Unclear, Get Used to It')." *Journal of American Studies* 36.2 (2002) 1–27.

Parry, Robin A. "The Ethics of Lament: Lamentations 1 as a Case Study." In *Reading the Law, Studies in Honor of Gordon J. Wenham*, edited by J. G. McConville and Karl Moller, 138–55. London: T. & T. Clark, 2007.

———. *Lamentations*. Two Horizons. Grand Rapids: Eerdmans, 2010.

———. "Lamentations and the Poetic Politics of Prayer." *Tyndale Bulletin* 62 (2011) 65–88.

———. "Prolegomena to Christian Theological Interpretations of Lamentations." In *Canon and Biblical Interpretation*, edited by Craig G. Bartholomew et al., 393–418. Grand Rapids: Zondervan, 2016.

———. "The Trinity and Lament." In *In Praise of Worship: An Exploration of Text and Practice*, edited by David J. Cohen and Michael Parsons, 143–61. Eugene, OR: Pickwick, 2010.

———. "Wrestling with Lamentations in Christian Worship." In *Spiritual Complaint: The Theology and Practice of Lament*, edited by Miriam J. Bier and Tim Bulkeley, 135–53. Eugene, OR: Pickwick, 2013.

Perkinson, James W. "Illin' the Evil, Outing the Absurd: Kierkegaardian Irony Meets Makavelian Grotesquery in the Postindustrial City." *Black Theology* 5 (2007) 355–78.

Pitts, Leonard. "The Distraction of Basketball Might Be Just What We Need." *Fort Worth Star-Telegram*, June 19, 2020.

———. "Trump's Many Lies No Longer Shock Us." *Fort Worth Star-Telegram*, September 14, 2020.

Poser, Rachel. "He Wants to Save Classics from Whiteness. Can the Field Survive?" *New York Times Magazine*, February 2, 2021.

Rambo, Shelly. *Resurrecting Wounds: Living in the Afterlife of Trauma*. Waco, TX: Baylor University Press, 2017.

Ramsay, Nancy J. "Moral Injury as Loss and Grief with Attention to Ritual Resources for Care." In *Military Moral Injury and Spiritual Care: A Resource for Religious Leaders and Professional Caregivers*, edited by Nancy J. Ramsay and Carrie Doehring, 142–68. St. Louis: Chalice, 2019.

Renkema, Johan. *Lamentations*. Historical Commentary on the Old Testament. Leuven: Peeters, 1998.

Roberts, Robert C. "Emotions among the Virtues of the Christian Life." *Journal of Religious Ethics* 20 (1992) 37–68.

———. *Emotions: An Essay in Aid of Moral Psychology*. Cambridge: Cambridge University Press, 2003.

———. "Emotions as Access to Religious Truths." *Faith and Philosophy* 9 (1992) 83–94.

———. *Emotions in the Moral Life*. Cambridge: Cambridge University Press, 2013.

———. *Spiritual Emotions: A Psychology of Christian Virtues*. Grand Rapids: Eerdmans, 2002.

———. *The Strengths of a Christian*. Philadelphia: Westminster, 1984.

———. "What an Emotion Is: A Sketch." *Philosophical Review* 97 (1988) 183–209.

———. "Will Power and the Virtues." *Philosophical Review* 93 (1984) 227–47.

Safren, Jonathan D. "'He Restoreth My Soul': A Biblical Expression and Its Mari Counterpart." In *Mari in Retrospect: Fifty Years of Mari and Mari Studies*, edited by Gordon D. Young, 265–71. Winona Lake, IN: Eisenbrauns, 1993.

Scarry, Elaine. *The Body in Pain*. Oxford: Oxford University Press, 1987.

Scott, James C. *Domination and the Arts of Resistance: Hidden Transcripts*. New Haven, CT: Yale University Press, 1990.

Sengal, Jesse. "On Endless Loop." *1843* magazine, April-May, 2020, 67–76.

Smith, Morton. "The Account of Simon Magus in Acts 8." In *Henry Austryn Wolfson Jubilee Volume on the Occasion of His Seventy-Fifth Birthday*, 2:735–49. Jerusalem: American Academy of Jewish Research, 1985.

Sölle, Dorothee. *Suffering*. Translated by Everett R. Kalin. Philadelphia: Fortress, 1975.

Sommer, Benjamin D. *A Prophet Reads Scripture: Allusion in Isaiah 40–66*. Contraversions. Stanford: Stanford University Press, 1996.

Stager, Lawrence E. "The Fury of Babylon: Ashkelon, and the Archaeology of Destruction." *Biblical Archaeology Review* 22.1 (1996) 56–69, 76–77.

Steiner, Claire-Antoinette. "L'écriture de l'inconsolable; le livre des Lamentations." *Foi et vie* 108 (2009) 7–18.

Sullivan, Jake. "Yes, America Can Still Lead the World." *Atlantic*, January/February 2019, 76–85.

Thomas, Heath Aaron. "Lamentations and the Trustworthiness of God." *Miqra* 7 (2008) 6–11.

Thurman, Howard. *Jesus and the Disinherited.* Nashville: Abingdon, 1949.

Tiemeyer, Lena-Sofia. "The Doubtful Gain of Penitence: The Fine Line between Lament and Penitential Prayer." In *Spiritual Complaint: The Theology and Practice of Lament,* edited by Miriam J. Bier and Tim Bulkeley, 105–24. Eugene, OR: Pickwick, 2013.

———. "Two Prophets, Two Laments and Two Ways of Dealing with Earlier Texts." In *Die Textualisierung der Religion,* edited by Joachim Schaper, 185–202. Tübingen: Mohr Siebeck, 2009.

Van Hecke, Pierre J. P. "Lamentations 3:1–6: An Anti-Psalm 23." *Scandinavian Journal of the Old Testament* 16 (2003) 264–82.

Viveiros, Nelia. Review of *The Body Keeps the Score: Brain, Mind, and Body in the Healing of Trauma,* by Bessel van der Kolk. *Journal of Loss and Trauma* 22 (2017) 167–69.

Wainwright, Elaine Mary. "Rachel Weeping for Her Children: Intertextuality, the Biblical Testaments and a Feminist Approach." In *A Feminist Companion to Reading the Bible—Approaches, Methods, and Strategies,* edited by Athalya Brenner-Idan and Carole R. Fontaine, 452–69. Sheffield, UK: Sheffield Academic, 1997.

Ward, Jesmyn. "On Witness and Respair: A Personal Tragedy Followed by Pandemic." *Vanity Fair,* September 2020.

Weddle, David L. "The Liberator or Exorcist, James Cone and the Classic Doctrine of Atonement." *Religion in Life* 49 (1980) 477–87.

West, Cornell. *Race Matters.* New York: Vintage, 1994.

Westermann, Claus. *Lamentations: Issues and Interpretation.* Edinburgh: T. & T. Clark, 1994.

———. *Praise and Lament in the Psalms.* Atlanta: John Knox, 1981.

Whitman, Walt. *Democratic Vistas.* In *The Portable Whitman,* edited by Mark Van Doren. New York: Penguin, 1945.

———. *Prose Works 1892.* Vol. 2. Edited by Floyd Stovall. New York: New York University Press, 1964.

Wilkinson, Margaret. Review of *The Body Keeps the Score: Brain, Mind, and Body in the Healing of Trauma* by Bessel van der Kolk. *Journal of Analytical Psychology* 61 (2016) 239–44.

Willey, Patricia Tull. *Remember the Former Things: The Recollection of Previous Texts in Second Isaiah.* SBLDS 161. Atlanta: Scholars, 1997.

Wolf, Hans Walter. *Anthropology of the Old Testament.* Philadelphia: Fortress, 1974.

Yansen, James W. W., Jr. *Daughter Zion's Trauma: A Trauma-Informed Reading of the Book of Lamentations.* Biblical Intersections 17. Piscataway, NJ: Gorgias, 2019.